THE BLACK COUNTRY
PAST & PRESENT

Black Country history is focused at an extremely local level. In 1914 the people of Hurst Hill erected a monument to their local benefactor, Dr Baker. When this was damaged by a motorist in 2002 the first reaction of City of Wolverhampton Council was that repairs were out of the question. The Hurst Hill (Coseley) Community Association and others protested and a piece of local history was saved. On 25 March 2002 Councillor Norman Davies joined the descendants of Dr Baker to unveil the restored memorial. *(Express & Star)*

THE BLACK COUNTRY PAST & PRESENT

NED WILLIAMS

WHSmith

First published in the United Kingdom in 2002 by
Sutton Publishing Limited exclusively for
WHSmith, Greenbridge Road, Swindon SN3 3LD

British Library Cataloguing in Publication Data
A catalogue record for this book is available from the British Library.

ISBN 0-7509-3132-9

Illustrations

Front endpaper: A coronation party in Turner Street, West Bromwich, 1953. *(Wilf Smith Collection)*
Back endpaper: The Harlequin Eagles set off from the Wakes Ground at the head of the Willenhall Carnival on Saturday 15 June 2002. The Parish Church of St Giles is in the background. *(Ned Williams)*
Half-title page: The Black Country has traditionally been associated with metal-working, and the Blackcountryman is often represented by the craftsman working at his forge. Here Mr Oswald Biddle produces ornamental iron work at Messrs Hill & Smith of Harts Hill in a picture once used in the Brierley Hill guide. *(Author's Collection)*
Title page: A book about the Black Country has to take into account its people as well as such things as landscape and industry. Like everyone else, Black Country folk celebrated the Golden Jubilee during 2002, and this all became entangled with World Cup interest and loyalties to local events. Willenhall's Jubilee Year Carnival on 15 June 2002 clashed with an England v Denmark football match – a great strain on loyalties! Teresa Merrideth and Trevor and Ian Gibbs from Bilston donned their Union Jacks to support the carnival and kept up with the match in the tea tent. *(Ned Williams)*

Typeset in 11/14pt Photina and produced by
Sutton Publishing Limited, Phoenix Mill,
Thrupp, Stroud, Gloucestershire GL5 2BU.
Printed and bound in England by
J.H. Haynes & Co. Ltd, Sparkford.

Contents

The Black Country Society was founded in 1967 and has played a key role in cultivating a regional approach to thinking about the area in which we live. The 1975 committee seen here includes such figures as Dr John Fletcher (President), John Brimble (Secretary) and Harold Parsons, who edited *The Blackcountryman* from 1967 to 1988. *(BCS Archives)*

The committee of the Black Country Society, 2002. The principal officers of the society are seated, left to right: Freda Allen (Secretary), Charles Hanmer (Chairman), Stan Hill (President and editor of *The Blackcountryman* from 1988 to 2001), Peter Skidmore (Treasurer) and Tony Copson (Vice Chairman). *(BCS Archives)*

Foreword

By Stan Hill, President of the Black Country Society

The term 'Black Country' was first used in the middle of the nineteenth century to describe the area of the South Staffordshire Coalfield where the Thick Coal, an amazing 30ft seam, came close to the surface. The 1850s and 1860s saw the peak of coal and iron production and the area would then have been at its blackest. In *All Around the Wrekin*, published by Chapman & Hall in 1860, Walter White wrote:

> . . . the Black Country. The name is eminently descriptive, for blackness everywhere prevails; the ground is black, the atmosphere is black, the underground is honeycombed by mining galleries stretching in utter blackness for many a league.

However, the term had no official status, and was not found on Ordnance Survey maps, for example. Indeed the Black Country was never given any precise boundaries, not even geological ones.

In an area of something over 150 square miles, about a hundred small industrial communities developed, and by the beginning of the twentieth century a couple of dozen of them, in their own right, or by linking with neighbours, were of sufficient size to become municipal authorities. Over the years there were several amalgamations of these units of local government, but it was the major local government reorganisations of 1966 and 1974 that left the area divided into four metropolitan boroughs: Walsall, Dudley, Sandwell and Wolverhampton. In marketing themselves to the rest of the world, these four boroughs gave recognition to the old regional name. As you entered any one of the boroughs, signs welcomed you to 'The Black Country'.

The Black Country Society was founded in 1967 as a reaction to the unstoppable moves towards larger units in all forms of human activity, and the fear that in this process our industrial heritage and the pride of local people would be swept away. A major aspect of the Black Country Society's work has been in the field of publishing. The Society's own quarterly magazine, *The Blackcountryman*, has printed over 2,000 authoritative articles about the area. The Society has also published over fifty books.

The coverage of the Black Country has been greatly expanded since 1994 through the Society's association with Sutton Publishing and its 'Britain in Old Photographs' series. Since then over fifty Black Country titles have been produced and over seventy thousand books sold, enabling us to share over ten thousand Black Country photographs with a wider audience.

We were glad that WH Smith joined this activity with titles exclusive to themselves, and we are pleased that two more local picture books are being produced to celebrate Golden Jubilee year. The two 'Past and Present' volumes on Wolverhampton and the Black Country, produced by one of the Society's members, provide another unique view of the area. The Society has never held that the region is best understood by simply looking at the past – our mission statement proclaims that we share an interest in the 'Past, Present *and Future*' of the area – and therefore I warmly recommend this work, and hope that it will promote a greater interest in the Black Country.

Stan Hill
Editor of The Blackcountryman *1988–2001, and Hon. President of the Society, 2001–2*

The Black Country has no civic or administrative identity and therefore we have no mayor, lord lieutenant or sheriff. After 1974 we were consigned to the West Midlands, a county which was never wholly ours and which no longer exists. For a century-wide contrast we have, therefore, turned to the Masons to provide us with two Provincial Grand Masters of Staffordshire. The Right Honourable William Legge, Earl of Dartmouth, became Provincial Grand Master of Staffordshire in 1893, two years after becoming Lord Lieutenant of the county. The Dartmouth family originally lived in West Bromwich, where they had considerable interests, but later moved to Patshull House, near Wolverhampton. *(Ian Bott Collection)*

The Right Honourable William Legge was Provincial Grand Master for forty years, but nowadays no one would expect to stay in such a post for such a length of time. The present Provincial Grand Master of Staffordshire is Mr Kevin Chawner, seen here. Mr Chawner has a background in retailing and comes from the Potteries. Ninety per cent of the Black Country has traditionally been in Staffordshire, but, of course, only forms a small part of that large county. Mr Chawner's province covers several distinct industrial areas based on coalfields plus huge rural districts. *(G.V. Jenkins LBIPP)*

Introduction

In 1921 a five-year-old boy from London came to live in the Black Country. He later described himself as fortunate to come to Rowley Regis at that time – a place where thirty pits were still at work, ironworks were in full production, canals were crowded with boats, and acres of derelict land provided a child's perfect adventure playground.

The young lad was J. Wilson Jones. He later became Rowley Regis librarian and in 1949 wrote *The History of the Black Country*. It is intriguing that in 1921 he was witnessing the end of an era in which the Black Country had stayed pretty much unchanged since the 1880s. Wilson Jones felt he had to write something about the area before it was all swept away.

Somebody arriving in the Black Country in the 1960s might have felt the same thing. It looked much as the 1930s had created it – and it was all about to change once more. So the truth is that whenever we first encounter the Black Country we are suddenly aware of its recent past, we have a sense of something changing, and an apprehension about what is coming next.

A millennium and a jubilee provide moments when the passing of time is given particular emphasis. Suddenly it seems relevant to ask how things have changed in the last hundred years, or how they have changed since Elizabeth II came to the throne. And what record do we possess of those changes? How does the past compare with the present? What has stayed the same? What has changed? Is it to our liking?

This book sets out to stimulate such questions through the use of photographs. Just skimming through these images emphasises impressions of both continuity and change. Some things are gone forever. The metal-working industries, the mining, the small independent townships, the style of people's lives – these things have changed or vanished. Others have simply been transmuted into a modern equivalent. What we think of as new might simply be something reinvented.

This book does not just look at the landscape, the industry and the townships of the Black Country. It also tries to examine the people themselves, by focusing on human activities like going to school, going shopping, and simply filling life outside work with all manner of strange activities, particularly in the quest for 'fun'. If this were not taken into account we would simply have produced a book that was full of 'past' pictures of pits, steelworks and town centres, contrasted with 'present' pictures of housing developments, industrial trading estates and shopping complexes.

Not many of the old photographs in this book were taken with the express purpose that sometime in the future they would be used in an exercise comparing then and now. They were taken simply to make an immediate record of the present, for sharing with others who were in the same present. We have taken them out of that context and given them historical significance by asking you to compare them with our new version of the present.

It is also true that the whole of the Black Country cannot really be summed in a couple of hundred photographs. Each one is just a representative of all the others that could not be included. We can't show you what every girl guide in the Black Country looked like in 1933 or 2002. We can't show you every street, every place of work, every source of entertainment. But we can show you something representative of this and that – and leave the rest to you! The Black Country is a fantastic place to explore, and exploring it with a camera, or with a pencil and notebook, is as socially exciting in 2002 as at any other time.

Ned Williams
August 2002

Black Country chaps and wenches. Ray Weston, on accordian, accompanies the famous Black Country choir 'Cum Sing Wi' We' at the Wolverhampton Vintage Transport Show on 25 May 2002. *(Ned Williams)*

Black Country chaps. Reuben Farley was born in West Bromwich in 1826, and began his career as an apprentice mining surveyor. After completing his apprenticeship he bought his own colliery! From then on his business interests grew and grew. When he died he was Chairman of Taylor & Farley Ltd, the Hamstead Colliery Co., Danks & Co. of Oldbury, Fellows, Morton & Clayton, the canal carriers, and the South Staffordshire Ironfounders' Association. However, since the age of eighteen he had also dedicated himself to 'public work' in education, local government and promotion of public utilities. He was Mayor of West Bromwich on several occasions and in 1896 became the first Freeman of that Borough. Although he remained a bachelor until the age of forty, he went on to marry three times. *(Ian Bott Collection)*

Tarsem King, Councillor Lord King of West Bromwich, was born in the Punjab in 1937. He came to Britain in 1960 and began working in the foundry industry before training as a teacher. He taught from 1968 until 1990, and has since become the managing director of his family business. He entered local politics and in 1992 became the first council leader of Indian origin in this country. In 1999 he was granted a life peerage as Lord King of West Bromwich. In 2001 he became Mayor of Sandwell. He is seen here with his wife Mohinder Kaur, dressed in their regalia as Mayor and Mayoress of Sandwell. *(Sandwell MBC)*

Black Country wenches. Dolly Allen (1906–90) was an outstanding Black Country performer. She recited her poetic monologues in the local dialect, capturing the bitter-sweet humour of the region, and was a popular performer in 'Black Country Night Out' shows. *(Ned Williams)*

Marlene Watson has preserved this tradition and updated it for today's audiences. She is seen here at a Chapel Anniversary Reunion in Quarry Bank on 12 May 2002. *(Ned Williams)*

Landscapes & Townscapes

This view looking towards Oldbury was taken just after the Second World War, at a time when clear views of the landscape were rare ('clean' air did not arrive until the 1960s). The picture was taken from one of the area's numerous tips, or 'bonks', and shows how industry, housing, canals and derelict land all seem to merge together to create a Black Country landscape. *(Author's Collection)*

Another Black Country landscape photographed just after the Second World War captures the modest scale of many Black Country pits – nearly all of which had stopped working by this time. These are believed to be the pits that were located just off Burton Road between Dudley and Upper Gornal, and which mined both fireclay and coal. *(Author's Collection)*

Returning to the site in 2002 we find that an industrial estate has been built across the bank on which the pits stood. The tall thin pipes rising from the ground are methane vents. They are to be found all over the Black Country where derelict land that was once mined has been relandscaped and reclaimed. Very little of the Black Country land surface can be described as 'natural' even when it's green. *(Ned Williams)*

The Coombs Wood Ironworks, *c*. 1910, from a John Price postcard. This is the view from the road that descends from Black Heath down Coombs Holloway into the valley of the River Stour. The works, which straddle the Dudley No. 2 Canal, seem to have carved their own shelf out of this valley. Later incorporated into the British Steel empire, the works became famous for producing tubes, but barely survived into the 1980s. *(BCS Archives)*

Today this landscape has been cleared and new factories and warehouses are springing up on the site, but it also boasts some of the most dramatic enclaves of open green space to be found in the whole region. Wonderful views can be had from the ground above the site of the works. The canal still threads its way through the site. *(Ned Williams)*

The Black Country lost its forests to the charcoal-burners and its only mountains are man-made. While its rivers are best forgotten, the greatest asset to the Black Country landscape is the canal system. The canal that made its way up into the Black Country from Birmingham in the 1760s truly made the local industrial revolution possible. Brindley's cut was improved by Smeaton and Telford, and this view at Deepfields Junction, near Bradley, marks the point where Brindley's original route leaves the wide straight cut made by Telford. In this view, taken on 16 August 1969, the adjacent main line railway and the chimneys of Bilston Steelworks can be seen. *(Michael Hale)*

In this more recent view the steelworks have vanished, the railway is obscured and the scene is dominated by the bridge carrying the Black Country Route over canal and railway. This road, linking the Wolverhampton–Birmingham road with the M6 at Junction 10, was opened by Neil Kinnock in 1995. *(David Hickingbottom)*

Not far from the location of the previous picture, the canal passed the Cannon Iron Foundry, pictured on 16 August 1969. The Cannon began life on this site in 1826 and remained there until the mid-1970s. In 1980 a fire destroyed most of the buildings, and what was left was demolished – all but a chimney which was eventually taken to the Black Country Museum. *(Michael Hale)*

The Cannon Foundry site was cleared and is now covered with new houses. The name survives in the Cannon Business Park built on the more recent Cannon Industries site in Gough Road, Coseley. One problem for a book such as this is that it could quite easily consist of nothing but pictures of yesterday's factories, followed by pictures of today's housing estates and business parks! *(Ned Williams)*

This picture was taken in July 1989 during the demolition of the works that had once been the home of Noah Hingley's famous chain and anchor works in Netherton. At the time demolition was quickly wiping out factories and works that had once been household names. Thousands of people had worked in the 'traditional' metal-bashing trades of the Black Country. Once again the Black Country landscape was going through a major metamorphosis. *(Ned Williams)*

Where Noah Hingley's factory once stood we now find the familiar landscape of the modern industrial estate – in this case the Washington Centre. Tree-lined access roads, neat forecourts, car parks and clean sheds abound but there is little sign of human activity. *(Ned Williams)*

Level Street, Brierley Hill, is one of the best places to see the dramatic changes through which the Black Country landscape has passed. In this 1980 view the road descends 'the levels' as it passes the Three Furnaces. A railway crossing used by the Earl of Dudley's Round Oak railway system can be seen at each level, and between these is a narrow canal bridge. Through the haze Netherton church can be seen on top of the hill rising above the roofs of the Enterprise Zone in the Blackbrook Valley. Every part of this land surface has been 'worked' by man, and with the closure of the Round Oak Steelworks things are about to change again. *(Keith Hodgkins)*

Today the Copthorne Hotel has replaced the Three Furnaces, the canal bridge has been widened and Level Street now makes a steady descent into the Merry Hill shopping complex. Netherton's church and the Rowley Hills still form the skyline. *(Ned Williams)*

This is the casting shop at the Round Oak Steelworks, Brierley Hill, on 8 December 1982 – two days before the final day of steel-making. As each of the Black Country's steelworks closed, difficult questions had to be faced concerning future jobs and prosperity, as well the future of the industrial sites. *(Keith Hodgkins)*

The Merry Hill shopping complex was not built directly on the site of the Round Oak Steelworks but its proximity compels us to see one as replacing the other. The modern shopping malls seen here in 2002 offer more than just a visual contrast to the picture above: they symbolise a shift away from the metal-based industries that made our landscape and defined the Black Country's identity. *(Ned Williams)*

This 1950s aerial view of the Round Oak Steelworks shows not just their massive size, but also their precise location in relation to Brierley Hill in the foreground – literally on the doorstep – and in relation to the much reworked territory beyond the works. It was this area that provided the space for the first stages of the Merry Hill development. *(Author's Collection)*

In 2002, as if by magic, the Merry Hill Centre is redefined as part of the town centre of Brierley Hill! Merry Hill is to the left, as indicated by the second sign, and the skyline is dominated by the Waterfront Development which borders the canal mentioned on p. 23. The question of what constitutes a 'town' is considered in the next few pages. *(Ned Williams)*

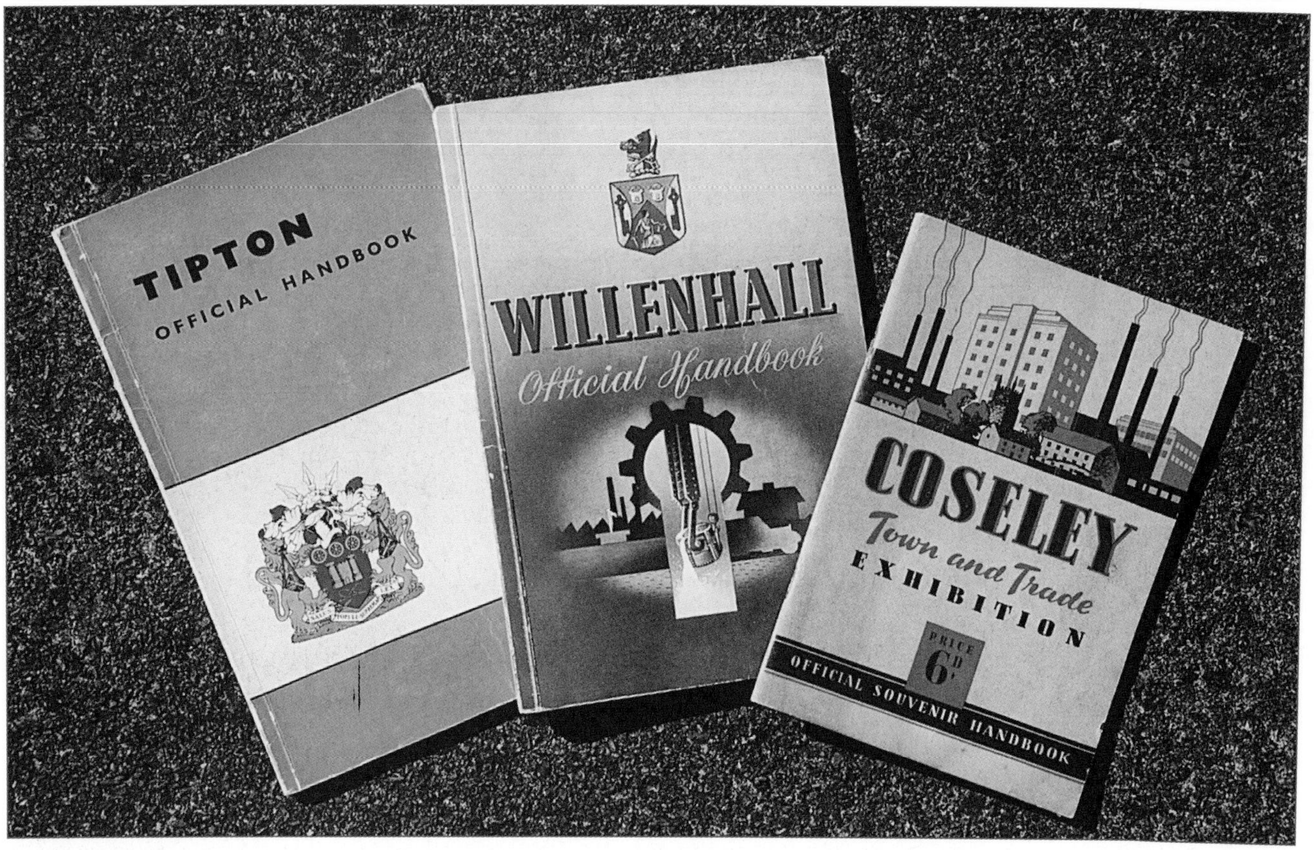

Black Country townships had grown so much during the nineteenth century that the emerging structures of local government had to recognise their identity and right to self-determination. Some urban districts, like Coseley and Willenhall, conducted their own affairs until reorganisation in 1966; others, like Tipton, were awarded borough status in the 1930s. The rationalisation of 1966 was mild compared with the events of 1974. *(Ned Williams)*

In 1974 local government boundaries changed again and we acquired the new metropolitan boroughs of Wolverhampton, Walsall, Sandwell and Dudley, and found ourselves in the county of the 'West Midlands'. While this may make administrative sense, it works against the Black Country tradition of seeing each component 'patch' of the region as intensely local. By 2002 Wolverhampton had become a city, Sandwell was searching for a new name, Walsall had almost succumbed to direct rule from Whitehall and Dudley faced an identity crisis! *(Ned Williams)*

In tandem with the landscape the Black Country's townscapes have also been changing. From the semi-abandoned arm of the Walsall Canal we look towards the centre of Walsall in 1980. Just in front of the 1960s office block is the ABC Cinema, still showing films on three screens, but it only lasted one more decade. *(Keith Hodgkins)*

In 2002 it is possible to gaze across the refurbished arm of the Walsall Canal towards the town centre. The cinema has been demolished and a Woolworth's built on the site. Interestingly, its outline is reminiscent of the theatre that occupied the site before the cinema! The scene is now dominated by Walsall's impressive new art gallery. *(Ned Williams)*

A trip along the A41 reveals towns trying to modernise while still hanging on to landmarks and mementoes of the past. Here we see a West Bromwich Corporation bus pausing at Carters Green by the Reuben Farley Memorial Clock Tower in the 1940s. The tower was built to express the gratitude of West Bromwich people to their benefactor Reuben Farley (*see* p. 15). *(Ken Rock Collection)*

Large buildings that once surrounded the clock tower at Carters Green, such as the church and the Tower Cinema, have now vanished. A new expressway guides traffic away from the High Street, but the tower still stands in splendid isolation to greet travellers intent on discovering the heart of West Bromwich in 2002. *(Ned Williams)*

The A41 originated as an early turnpike road that became part of the national road system when it was incorporated into Telford's route from London to Holyhead. It passes through a variety of Black Country communities. Hill Top, halfway between West Bromwich and Wednesbury, is a place that can easily be overlooked. The road looks quiet in this 1950s view. *(Ian Bott Collection)*

In 2002 little seems to have changed, although the road is usually full of traffic! On closer inspection it can be seen that the buildings flanking the road have completely changed. *(Ned Williams)*

The Holyhead road avoided the centre of Wednesbury with its attractive market place laid out around the clock tower. The latter was built and inaugurated in 1911 to mark the coronation of King George V. The market was moved to a new location in 1970. *(Ian Bott Collection)*

Like its fellow 'steel towns' Brierley Hill and Bilston, Wednesbury seemed to be in danger of fading away in the 1980s. The Black Country Development Corporation put money into propping up the town's ailing centre and some regeneration was effective. In a world in which everything from work to shopping has changed, these centres need to find a new lease of life. *(Ned Williams)*

Next stop along the A41 is Bilston, another town much affected by the demise of its local steelworks. A proud independent borough from 1933 to 1966, it should have realised that the trolleybuses were already bringing it within the orbit of Wolverhampton! Here a trolleybus emerges from Bilston Depot shortly before the Bilston routes were abandoned in 1964/5. *(Clifford Brown/John Hughes Collection)*

In the mid-1920s, when Wolverhampton was trying to abandon its tramway system in favour of trolleybuses and was attempting to acquire privately owned local tramways, Bilston Urban District Council asserted its independence by opposing the plans. The tramways centred on this depot and the depot itself were finally municipalised in 1928. Looking down Mount Pleasant in 2002 it is interesting to note that the Wolverhampton & District Tramway Company's office has survived with its frontage intact. *(Ned Williams)*

Dudley occupies a special position in the heart of the Black Country. This Edwardian postcard view shows the 'entrance' to Dudley with the old version of the Station Hotel on the left and Dudley's wonderful Opera House on the right. Beyond are the wooded slopes of Castle Hill, then in Staffordshire although the rest of Dudley was in Worcestershire! *(Ken Rock Collection)*

In the 1930s Castle Hill saw major redevelopment. The Station Hotel was rebuilt and the Odeon and Plaza cinemas opened on opposite sides of the road. The zoo on Castle Hill opened in 1937 and the Opera House burnt down in the same year – to be replaced by the Hippodrome seen in this 2002 view. The area has now been christened Castle Gate and controversial plans are afoot to remodel the 'gateway' to Dudley. *(Ned Williams)*

The Black Country is also awash with villages, most of which have clearly defined centres like the one seen here in Sedgley. The Bull Ring was photographed on 9 January 1902, the day the electric trams began operating between Wolverhampton and Dudley. The church spire is a well-known landmark that can be seen for miles. *(The Robinson Collection)*

The buildings on the right in the picture above were demolished in about 1935 to make way for the new Clifton Cinema which opened on 17 May 1937. This picture was taken in September 1997 from the old projection room of the Clifton just as the building was being converted to a pub. The turnpike route to Dudley lies straight ahead – the older route had followed the Ridgeway and left Sedgley via the narrow street seen in the top picture. *(Ned Williams)*

On a smaller scale various types of building – pubs, shops, houses, cinemas, churches and garages – have also witnessed dramatic changes. For a start, the most sacred of Black Country buildings – the public house – is now found in smaller numbers. This picture of the Spread Eagle in Darlaston in the early 1900s shows a typically unpretentious local pub. Mr M.P. Foster, the landlord, also found time to be a file-cutter in the gun trade. The building was demolished in the 1950s. *(Eileen Beards Collection)*

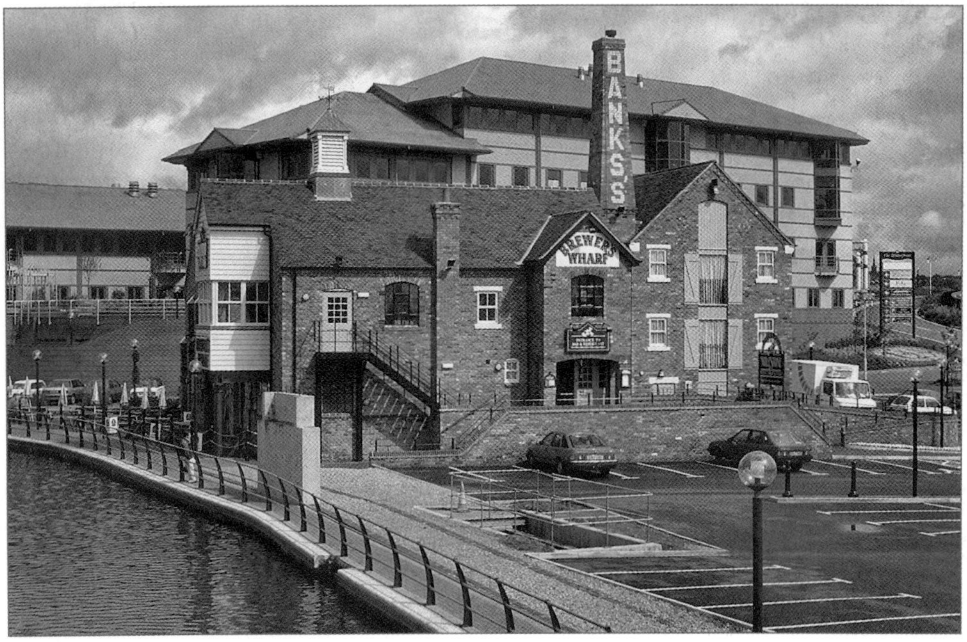

At the beginning of the twenty-first century we can survey Wacky Warehouses, real ale pubs, theme pubs, restaurant pubs, a few traditional pubs and even a few piles of rubble where some great pubs have fallen. In the 1990s the shiny new world of Merry Hill opted for a new 'old' pub: the Brewers Wharf. *(Ned Williams)*

Prince's End post office was run by Joseph Brain, pictured here in 1908. When he died in 1936 his daughter Nellie took over. When she died in 1951, Miss Watts, who had worked for Nellie, took over and ran the post office until 1970. *(Ken Rock Collection)*

The Caledonia post office, Quarry Bank, serves an area that takes its name from the Caledonia clay which was mined locally. Eddy Mattocks and his wife Pat are calling at the post office on 8 July 2002 to collect his first pension payment. Sub-post offices are seen as a vital component in the delivery of a variety of local services. *(Ned Williams)*

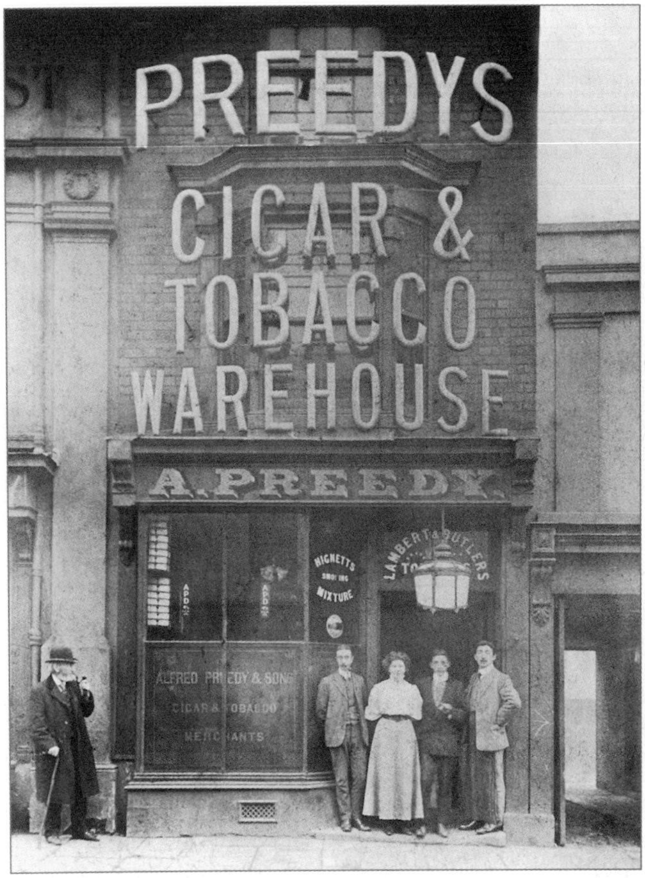

The typical Victorian shopfront of Preedy's tobacconist at 38 Market Place, Dudley, 5 November 1908. Note the pipe smoker gazing at the staff! *(Ken Gough Collection)*

Many Victorian shopfronts were swept away in areas like Dudley's Market Place in the 1960s. However, in 2002 it is still possible to buy tobacco at this location although the shop is part of the Dillons chain. *(Ned Williams)*

Through its branch structure the Co-operative Society was once able to maintain a presence in every community of any size. Here is Branch 9 of the Halesowen & Hasbury Co-operative Society at Wollaston, shortly after its opening on 21 March 1929. Like all the Society's local branches it was designed by Stanley Beach of Halesowen. *(Midland Co-operative Society Collection)*

These substantial buildings survived long after the demise of the Co-operative Society and Branch 9 still stands in Wollaston as the Wollaston Bathroom Centre. *(Ned Williams)*

The Holly Hall branch of the Dudley Co-operative Society, photographed soon after its opening in 1923, when all the 'hands' were male but each branch had a female cashier. These branches were closed when the Dudley Society was taken over by the Birmingham Society in 1982, although a family-owned general store still operates on the site. *(Author's Collection)*

Co-operative societies have merged into ever larger units, but have now begun to open small supermarkets to meet local needs, rather than simply building more hypermarkets. The new branch of the Midlands Co-operative Society on Milking Bank, Dudley, opened in September 2000 in an area of new housing. *(Ned Williams)*

The local shops that do survive tend to be modernised or operate in new buildings. Thus we have lost many of the local stores of character. The 'Tin Shop' in Darby's End, Netherton, seen here in the 1980s, was a distinctive corrugated iron building. *(Ned Williams)*

Gradually the shop was modernised and extended until its corrugated iron exterior completely disappeared. Looking at this 2002 view it is difficult to imagine that one building grew into the other. The nearest bus stop is still called the 'Iron Schools' in reference to other local corrugated iron buildings which seem to have become something of a legend. *(Ned Williams)*

Sedgley's Garage, Lawrence Lane, Old Hill, *c.* 1973. In those days petrol pumps still looked like petrol pumps and an attendant came to serve you! This is believed to have been the first garage/filling station in Old Hill. The attendant's hut is on the left. The buildings on the right were used by a wheelwright. *(Dave Whyley)*

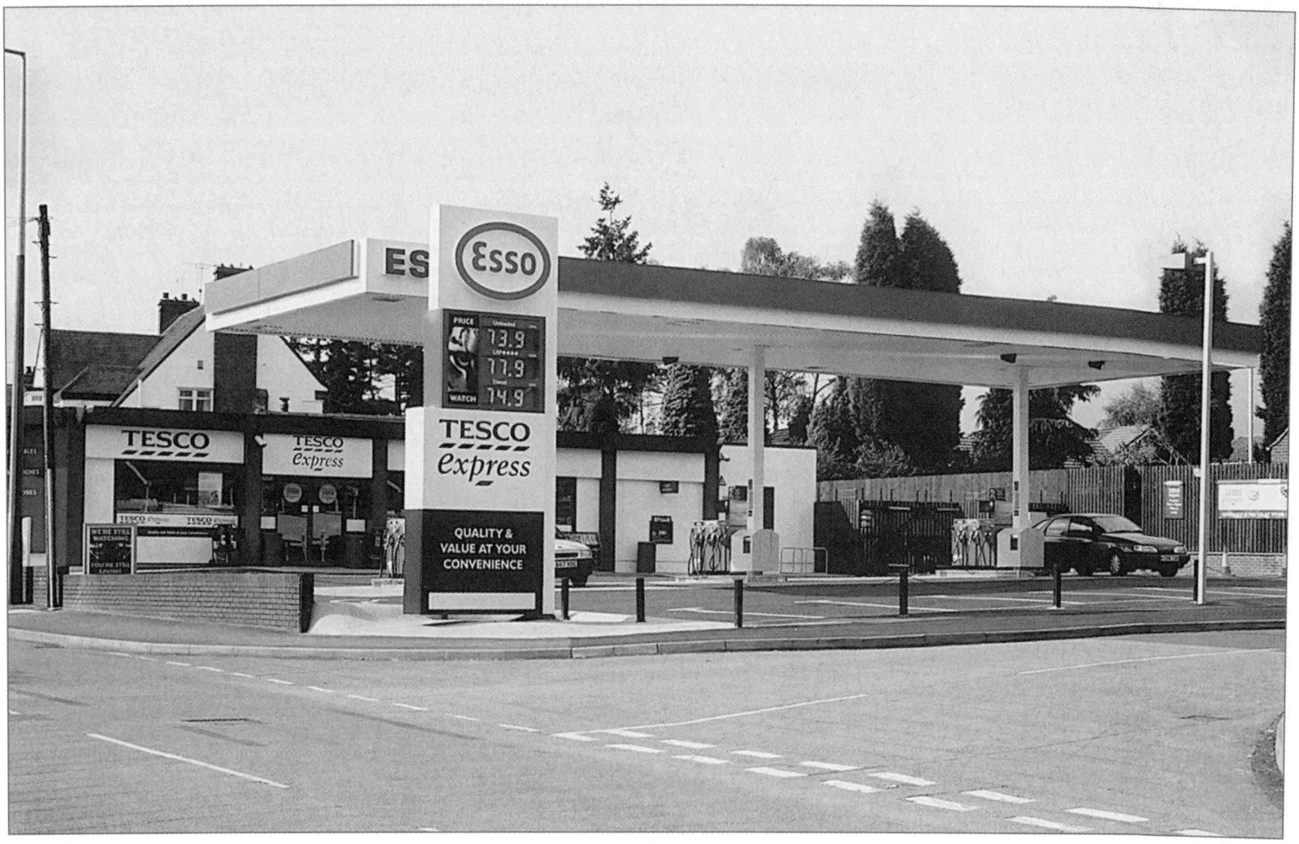

Latest-generation filling stations try hard to be local supermarkets as well. The new Esso/Tesco Express opened in Kingswinford in the spring of 2002. The supermarket was quickly assembled on site from a kit – the modern equivalent of the corrugated iron buildings that were once supplied in kit form. *(Ned Williams)*

The Halesowen & Hasbury Co-operative Society's new model dairy, seen here in 1932, was the organisation's pride and joy when it opened in Halesowen. It was located alongside the new 'Model Bakery' and four managers' houses were built behind the site so that the managers could walk out of their back gardens to work. *(Midlands Co-operative Society Collection)*

Today McDonald's occupies the site, and the fence at the back of the car park no longer has gates into the gardens of the 'Co-op' houses beyond. *(Ned Williams)*

These terraced houses built close to the canal in Tipton were typical of the late nineteenth-century housing found in every Black Country town. Even back in 1947, when this picture was taken, planners felt they had had their day. Interestingly, though, many survive. *(Author's Collection)*

In recent years canalside locations have been seen in a more positive light. This area, developed in partnership with the Black Country Development Corporation, includes a brand new basin to maximise canal frontage for the houses at Tividale Quays. ('Wharf' rather than 'quay' is the usual Black Country term!) *(Ned Williams)*

Joe Russell took this photograph of Soho Street, Smethwick, in the mid-1960s as he watched streets of terraced housing being replaced with new high-rise blocks of flats. *(Joe Russell Collection)*

The flats have now been occupied for thirty-five years and some of their contemporaries have been demolished! Soho Street has become Soho Close, and Soho House now stands where the terrace of houses and shops once stood. *(Ned Williams)*

Joe Russell was a local man who took the trouble to record photographically the changes through which his part of the Black Country was going in the 1960s. His pictures record vanishing terraces of houses and corner shops. When he took this picture at West Smethwick in 1968 he probably thought the new multi-storey flats were part of a new world that was here to stay. However, the scene has changed entirely. The tower block has been demolished, the station has closed and the industrial skyline (The 'Birmid') has disappeared. *(Joe Russell)*

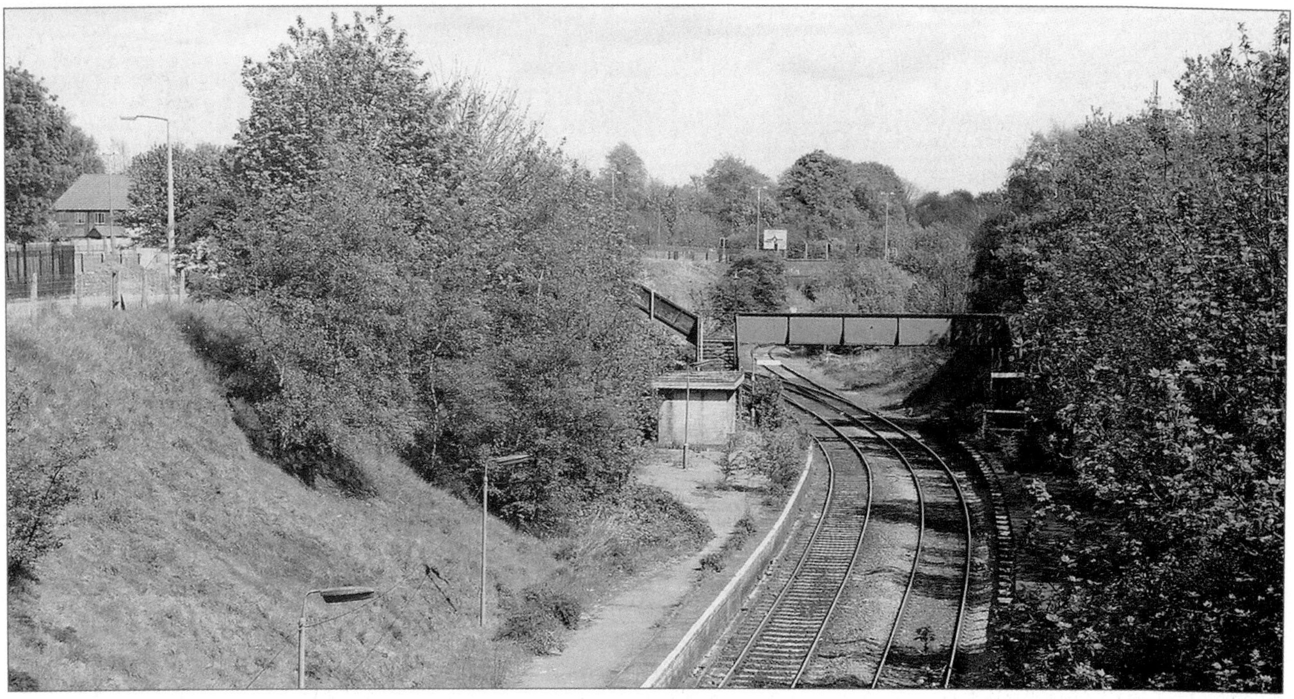

This 2002 view was taken from the same railway bridge as the above picture. Smethwick West station has closed and the tower block has gone. The railway tracks are still very much in use, but most trains now take the restored line from here to Birmingham Snow Hill (The Jewellery Line) and use a new station called Galton Bridge. *(Ned Williams)*

During the nineteenth century the number of churches in the Black Country greatly increased to keep up with the rising population figures. Within the Church of England parishes had to be divided and sub-divided from the 1840s onwards. St Stephen the Martyr's in Wolverhampton Street, Willenhall, was consecrated in 1845 but was eventually defeated by dry rot. *(Church Collection)*

Below: A new church dedicated to St Stephen the Martyr was built, and was opened by the Right Reverend Barry Rogerson, then Bishop of Wolverhampton, on 8 September 1979. This picture was taken on 14 July 2002 as the vicar, the Revd Graham Bennett, and early arrivals wait for the rest of the congregation to materialise. These pictures nicely contrast nineteenth- and twentieth-century church architecture. *(Ned Williams)*

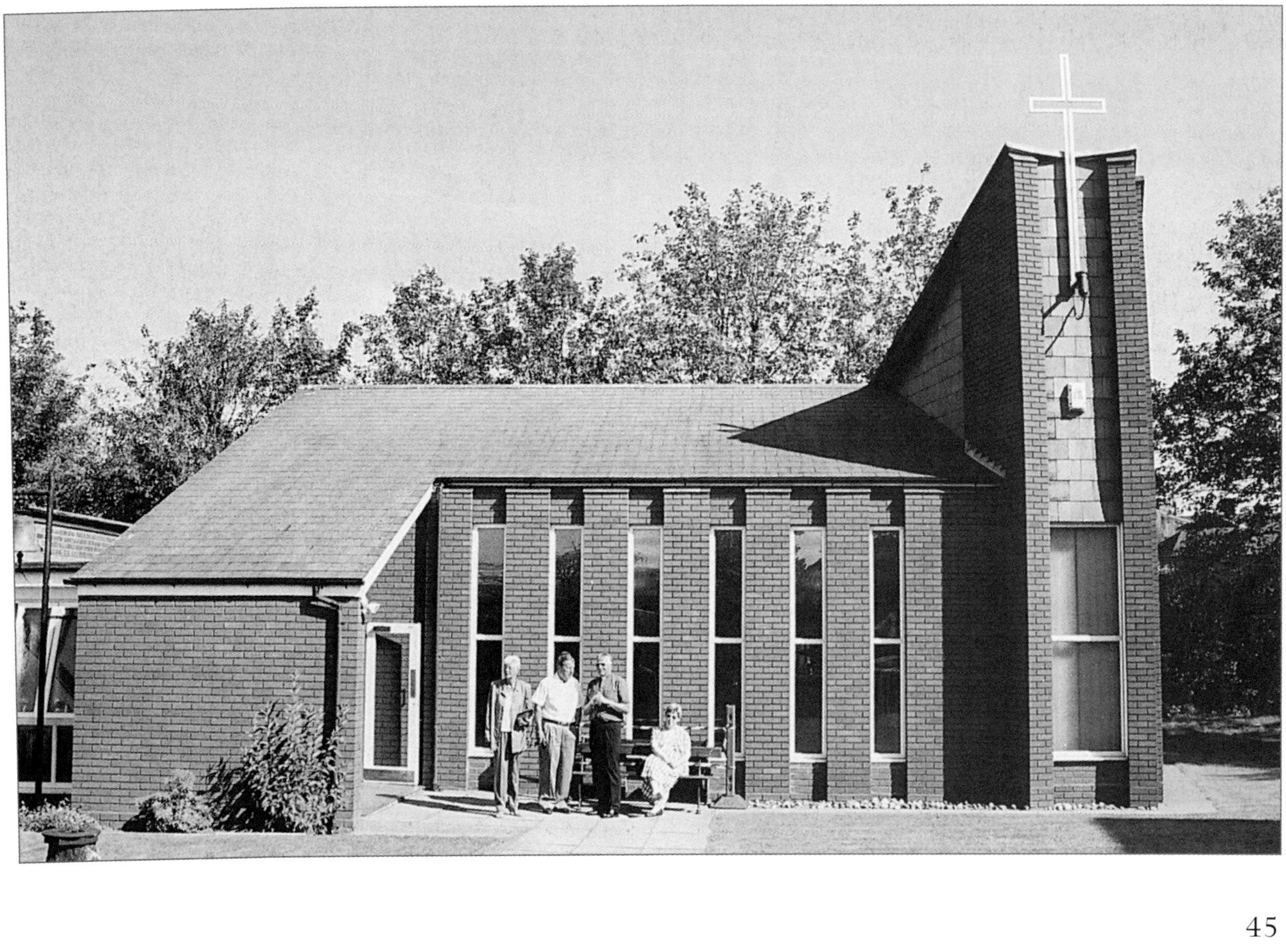

The Odeon in Dudley was opened on 28 July 1937 and was a fine example of the style of building developed by the Odeon circuit, now much-loved by fans of 1930s architecture and design. This picture was taken in 1952 when the cinema was fifteen years old. It closed in February 1975 and the future of the building, occupying a key site on Dudley's Castle Hill, seemed uncertain. *(Joe Alexander Collection)*

It was rescued by the Jehovah's Witnesses in 1976 and since then it seems to have gone through continual refurbishment and improvement. This photograph of the interior was taken in January 2002 after the latest major refit. It is now better than it was originally! Small faults in the detailing, perhaps the result of economies in the 1930s, are now put right and the whole is completed to a more consistent overall standard. *(Ned Williams)*

Growing Up & Going to Church

Young Clara Bott proudly displays her doll's pram outside her family's shop in Camp Street, Wednesbury, in 1927. *(Ian Bott Collection)*

The Black Country Living Museum has recreated the style and atmosphere of the late nineteenth-century schoolroom – which survived well into the twentieth century. The pupils are reciting their tables in the reconstructed school building that was once St James' School, Eve Hill, Dudley. It closed in 1989 and 'reopened' at the museum in 1992. *(Ned Williams)*

At Charlemont Junior School, West Bromwich, on 20 May 2002, we find these Year Six children not in a classroom but in an 'Independent Learning Zone', fully equipped with computers and its walls decorated in an astronomical theme. This room stands between two classrooms that bear little resemblance to that shown above. *(Ned Williams)*

Mr Bissell with his class at Charlemont Junior School half a century ago. *(Ian Bott Collection)*

Strangely enough it is possible to return to the same playground in the spring of 2002 and take much the same kind of picture. The teachers, Miss Shingler and Miss Smith, line up with pupils from the two Year Six classes who left Charlemont in the summer of 2002 to go on to secondary schools. *(Ned Williams)*

Girls at St Joseph's Roman Catholic Secondary School in Dudley, *c.* 1951. The buildings have since been demolished and the school itself absorbed into the large Bishop Milner School on the Sedgley side of Dudley. The 1944 Education Act set out to create three types of secondary state education: grammar, technical and modern schools. The only complications to the tri-partite system were that any of these types of school could also be categorised as 'co-ed' or 'single sex', and some were denominational schools. *(Mary Stevens)*

By the beginning of the twenty-first century secondary education had become extremely complicated: community colleges, centres of excellence, city academies, technical high schools are all keen to blow their own trumpets – alongside single-sex schools, mixed schools, religious schools and even 'bog-standard' comprehensives. Here members of the St Peter's Collegiate School Concert Band from Wolverhampton make themselves heard on 7 July 2002. *(Ned Williams)*

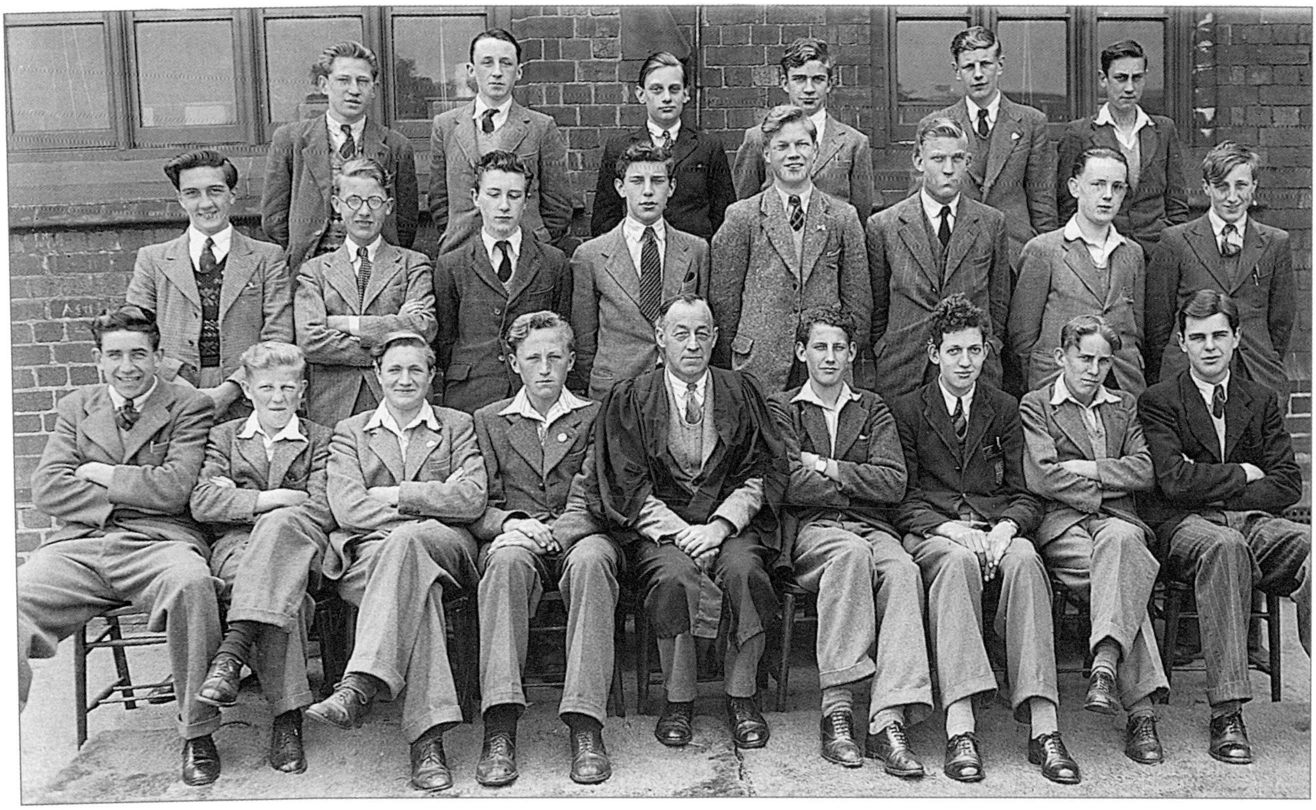

The King Edward VI College in Stourbridge was a boys' grammar school from 1552 until 1976 when it decided to become a co-educational sixth form college. In 1949 senior boys of the school sat down for this formal photograph with Mr Featherstone. *(Judith Hyde Collection)*

The atmosphere of a modern mixed sixth form college is captured in this informal picture taken in the courtyard at break. During 2002 the college celebrated its 450th anniversary. *(Jeremy Panko)*

Charley Aston (senior altar boy) and David Tibbetts lead Father Tuite (left) and parish priest Father Quilty (right) in the May Church Procession of 1952 at Our Blessed Lady and St Thomas of Canterbury Church, which happens to be in St Joseph's Road, Dudley. *(David Tibbetts)*

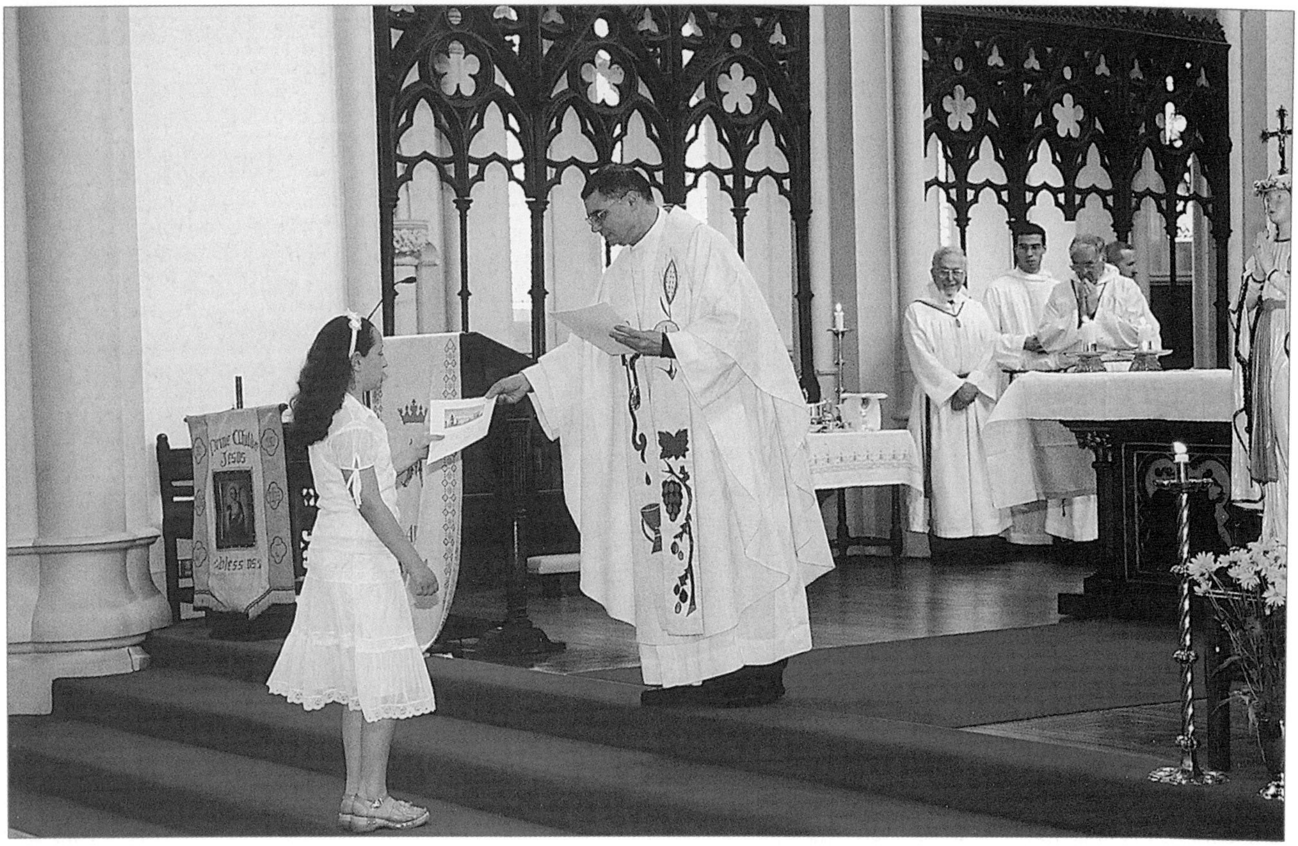

First communion: Father Emanuel hands out a certificate to a new communicant at St Mary's & St John's Church, Wolverhampton, on 26 May 2002. The girls still wear white dresses and the boys wear red sashes. The most popular tradition seems to be that everyone sits down afterwards to a communion breakfast. *(Ned Williams)*

In the 1960s Sunday schools could still muster enough folks to put on a parade and a good display of banners. Here we see Swan Bank Methodist Church Sunday School of Bilston out on the streets. *(Harold Dale)*

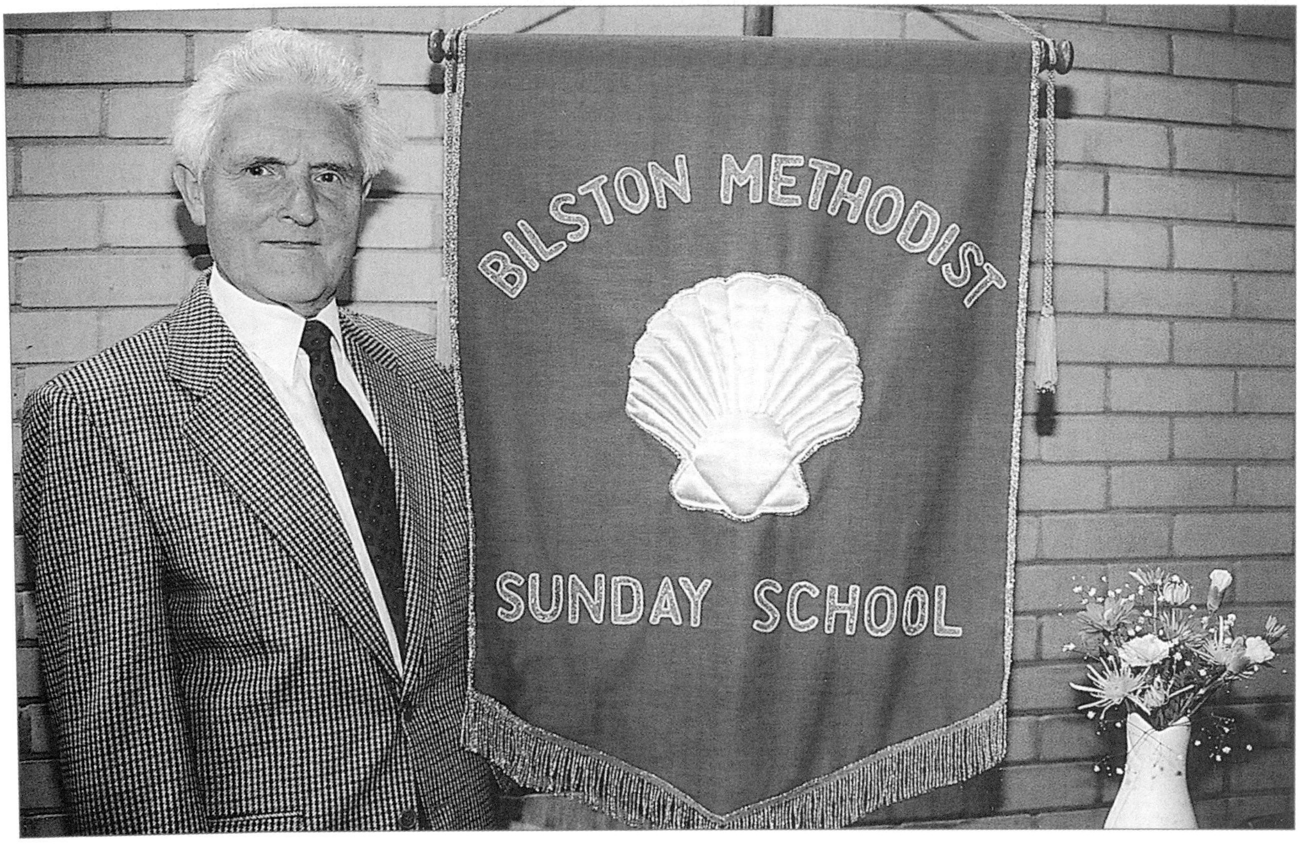

The same banner is still to be found in the Swan Bank Methodist Church but it is no longer seen on the streets of Bilston. Tony Hupperdine, a Sunday school teacher for forty years, presents the banner on 23 June 2002 when the Scouts were celebrating their twenty-fifth anniversary at the church. *(Ned Williams)*

The Sunday School anniversary at Upper Ettingshall (Sodom) Methodist Church in 1977. Note the abundance of pupils – but even then there were fewer than in pre-war days. The minister is the Revd J. Barrett. *(Jennifer Hill)*

There were eleven children present at the Upper Ettingshall Church in May 2000. *(Jennifer Hill)*

Sunday School pupils and members of the congregation at Hurst Hill Methodist Church pose for the camera in 1910 during the ceremony held to lay the foundation stone for a new Sunday school building. *(Church Collection)*

Hurst Hill Methodist Church celebrated its 200th anniversary on 30 June 2002. Organiser Pam Hughes (centre) is flanked by seven Sunday school children: Sam Thomas, Adam Massey, Linzi McFarlane, April Ashton, Emily Nelson, George Powell and Thomas Massey, plus the choir and musicians. Just in front of the banner are the guest minister John Sadler and the organist Graham Hancox. *(Ned Williams)*

Members of the Hurst Hill Mutual Improvement Class in 1928, photographed in Rock Road Recreation Ground which belonged to the church. These people gave up Saturday evenings to attend class. *(Church Collection)*

The Hurst Hill Methodist Church still has its Sunday school banner, proudly displayed on the church's 200th anniversary on 30 June 2002. *(Ned Williams)*

Members of the Willenhall Salvation Army Corps assemble on the stage of the hall behind their new citadel in 1984, celebrating their 100th anniversary. *(Mary Fowler Collection)*

Members of the Willenhall Salvation Army congregation assemble in the same hall in July 2002. *(Ned Williams)*

The Salvation Army came to Willenhall in 1881, and from 1884 to 1962 had a wooden citadel in Moat Street. When this was destroyed by fire it was replaced with a new building in Field Street, seen here as it was opened on 20 June 1970 by Mr Eger, of Josiah Parkes Ltd. *(Mary Fowler Collection)*

In 2002 the Salvation Army Corps in Willenhall is led by Captains Steve and Jenny Forman, seen here with their children in front of the Blood and Fire badge which adorns the front of the Field Street Citadel. *(Ned Williams)*

The Black Country at Work

Black Country collieries were relatively small until the twentieth century brought the sinking of deeper and larger pits. Pictures therefore exist in which the entire workforce at a pit seems to have assembled for the occasion. These colliers worked in the Cottage Street pit, Brierley Hill, in the early 1920s. *(Benjamin Jones)*

Baggeridge Colliery was one of several deep pits opened 'outside' the Black Country (in the sense that they were sunk beyond the 'boundary faults'). Exploration in the area began in the 1890s but the pit did not begin full production until 1912. The winding frame, engine house, screens and associated buildings were much more impressive than those at the smaller pits, as seen in this 1930s picture. *(Author's Collection)*

Below: Baggeridge Colliery ceased production on 1 March 1968. Thirty years later, in 1998, retired miners came to a reunion at the Baggeridge Country Park to witness the unveiling of this statue. Although the brickworks associated with the pit is still in operation the rest of the colliery site has been turned into landscaped parkland. *(Ned Williams)*

Giovanni Terrazzino came to Britain from Italy in 1951 on a four-year contract with the National Coal Board. After three months' initial training he was consigned to Baggeridge Colliery, where he is pictured. Many Italian workers disliked the work and left the mines for employment in foundries and steelworks. *(Anna Casa Collection)*

Derek Saunders, a park ranger, surveys the former colliery site from his office in the summer of 2002. Some members of his family had worked in the Jubilee and Hamstead Collieries, near West Bromwich, but mining was not in his blood so he went into the forging industry making aerospace components before coming to Baggeridge Country Park ten years ago. *(Ned Williams)*

Many industries associated with the Black Country have vanished or changed beyond recognition. The glass industry, which once dominated the area between Brierley Hill and Stourbridge, now exists only to 'finish' glassware made elsewhere and as a tourist attraction. Stan Gill is seen here making a ceremonial goblet at the Stuart Crystal factory in 1974. *(Sylvia Gill Collection)*

The Red House glass cone at Wordsley has been beautifully restored and the works now form part of a tourist trail. It was formally opened as a visitor centre on 26 July 2002 by Sir William Lawrence, chairman of the Heart of England Tourist Board. *(Ned Williams)*

Each Black Country town developed a specialisation within the metal trades – tubes from Wednesbury, locks from Willenhall, chains from Netherton and Cradley Heath, galvanised ironware from Quarry Bank and the Lye, and so on. Wednesfield specialised in traps. Here we see Ted Tonks with the lion traps made at Sidebothams up until the late 1950s. These traps were a good example of a locally made product designed, of course, for export. All kinds of products from chains to railway bridges made their way to markets all over the world. *(Ted Tonks Collection)*

Below: Some trades are now 'preserved' in local museums like Willenhall's wonderful Lock Museum. Others are represented at the Black Country Living Museum. Here we see Sidebotham's Trap Works, faithfully recreated at the museum. *(Ned Williams)*

Black Country chaps at work. The lead burners, including Charlie Price, Ted Wilson, Sammy Hadley and Bill Hart, are putting the finishing touches to the top of a lead chamber at the chemical plant belonging to Messrs Chance & Hunt at Oldbury in the 1950s. *(Charlie Price Collection)*

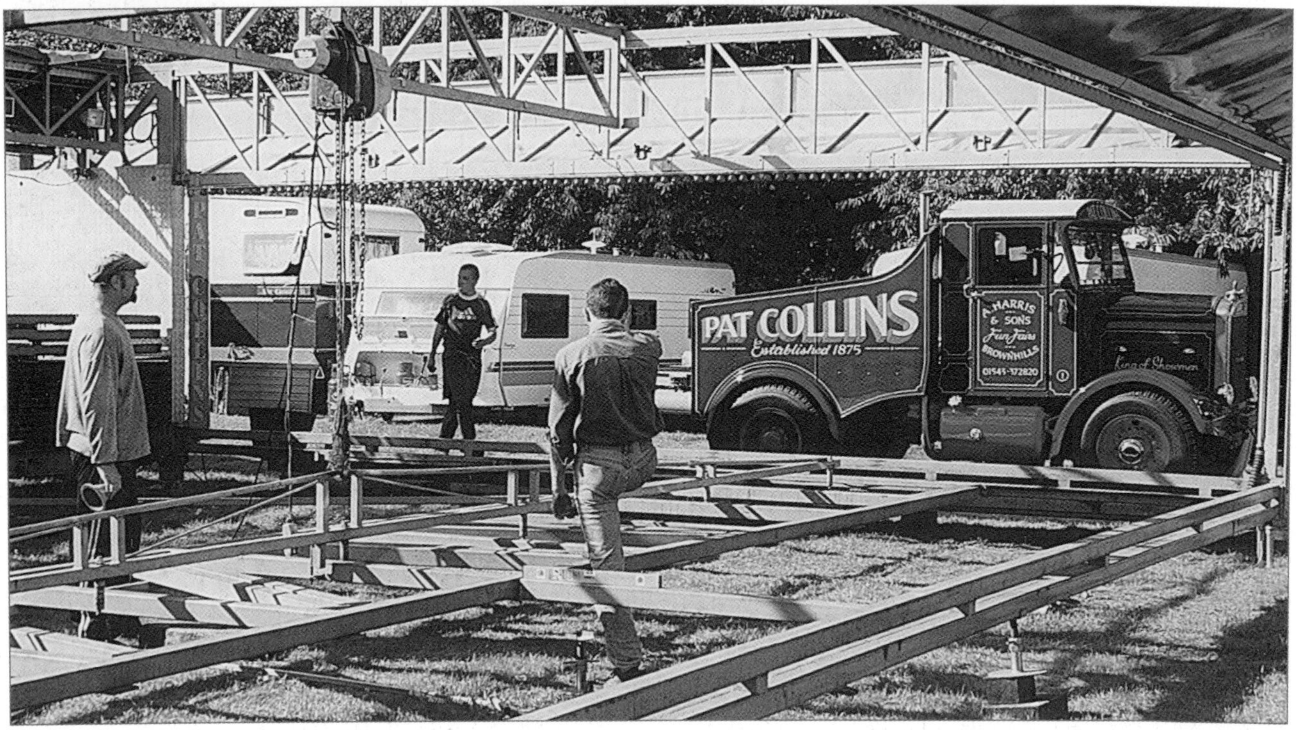

Where do you find chaps 'grafting' in the twenty-first century? Try visiting your local fairground while the build-up is in progress. Here we see Pat Collins' men building up the dodgems in Hickman Park, Bilston, in August 2001 in preparation for 'Bilston on Sea'. Assisted by hydraulics and electric hoists the men still have to manoeuvre large aluminium components into place and keep everything level. *(Ned Williams)*

Black Country wenches at work. Women workers on semi-automatic presses making nuts and bolts and accessories for the aerospace industry at Rubery Owen, Darlaston, in the mid-1950s. The long Black Country tradition of women undertaking industrial work was reinforced during both world wars. Women have also, therefore, been affected by de-industrialisation. *(Author's Collection)*

When new jobs are announced in the Black Country it is often the case that they are aimed at women, and particularly women prepared to work part-time. Donna Evans and her staff take a break from making sandwiches and selling cakes at the Firkin's Bakery in Quarry Bank in the spring of 2002. *(Ned Williams)*

A grand line-up of drivers, conductors, managers and lads at a steam tram depot in West Smethwick, *c.* 1900. The depot belonged to the Birmingham & Midland Tramways Ltd. Services were electrified in 1904. *(Angela Russell Collection)*

Bus drivers working for Travel West Midlands pause for a break at Walsall's new bus station in the summer of 2002. *(Ned Williams)*

Edward Hickey, an apprentice tool-maker at Josiah Parkes of Willenhall, setting a lever-springing machine in 1961. Like all young engineers, he was confident that he would never have to do anything else, and that engineering was a way of life that would last forever. He later became a probation officer. *(Edward Hickey Collection)*

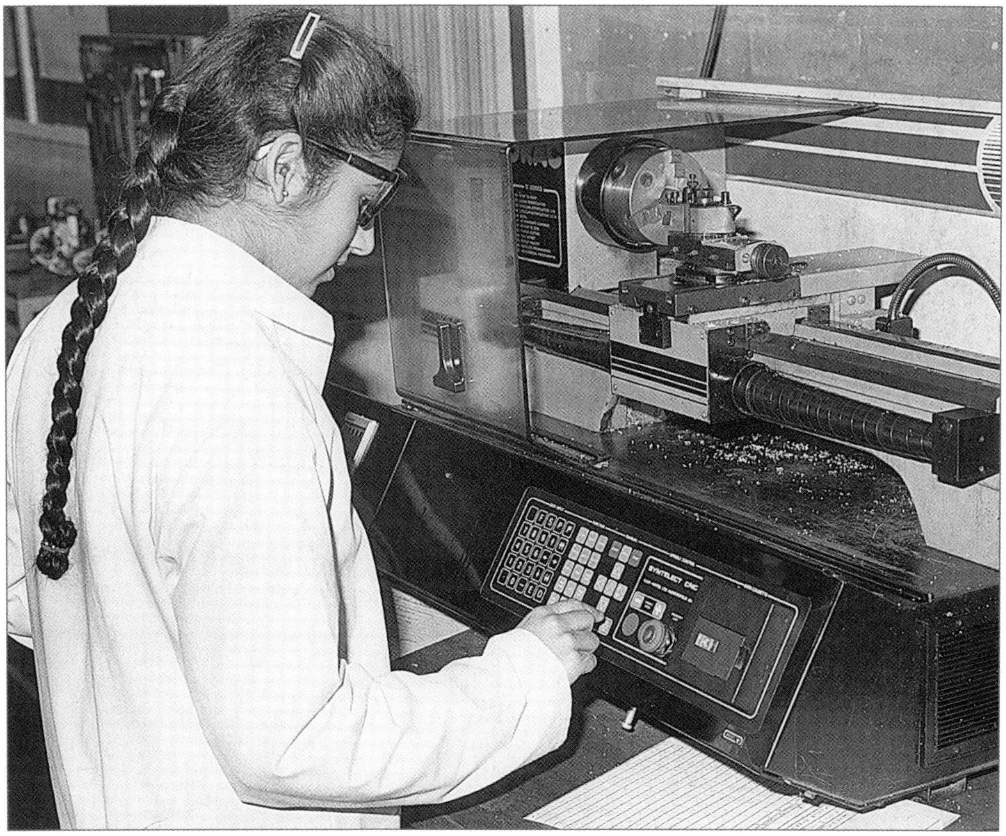

Paramjit Kaur, on a Women's Technician Training Scheme in Wolverhampton in the 1990s, works with CNC equipment. *(City of Wolverhampton College)*

When it comes to work, what counts is knowing what you really want to do. Young Kerry Foley of West Bromwich attends a visiting circus in 1982 and immediately knows what she wants to do – and makes a friend for life. *(Barry Foley Collection)*

Kerry gained qualifications in Business Administration before she joined the circus – to be as useful out of the ring as in it. She is seen here with the clown Alexis while working with Zippo's Circus – with whom she travelled to West Bromwich! She now works with Gilbert & Paulo's Circus, mainly travelling in the south of England. *(D. Andre)*

Staff at Barclays Bank, Bilston, *c.* 1957. Present are Olwyn Simkin (cashier/typist), Margaret Woodhall (clerk), Janet Hickman (junior) and Peter Davies (junior). Although one didn't go to work dressed casually, a dress code was implemented in order to express the corporate image of the organisation. *(Margaret Woodhall Collection)*

When Sadia Naz and Dave Price dress for work at the Dartmouth Square branch of the West Bromwich Building Society in 2002, they know their appearance is part of projecting the corporate image of their employer. While many banks have gone global, some building societies have managed to preserve their local identity as well as mutuality. The West Bromwich Society, which is involved in the life of the local community, celebrated its 150th anniversary in 1999. *(WBBS)*

The librarian issues a book to a borrower in Wednesbury Central Library in 1950. Both avoid eye contact and the transaction is completed in silence! The library opened in October 1908 and is a typical Black Country example of buildings benefiting from the munificence of Andrew Carnegie. *(Wednesbury Library Collection)*

You are likely to encounter a very different atmosphere in a library in 2002. Here, some of the staff at Wednesbury Library line up for the opening of a new Learning Centre on 21 May 2002. Present are Tracy Pozzar, Nicola Brightman, Hema Patel, Josie Badger and Claude Fraser. Modern libraries issue audiotapes and videotapes, and provide access to the Internet. Even borrowing books is not unknown! *(Ned Williams)*

On the Move

It was the canal system that really got the Black Country on the move at the end of the eighteenth century. Two hundred years later commercial traffic on the local canals had almost disappeared, but this mid-1960s photograph shows a coal boat moored at Short Heath Basin on the Wyrley & Essington Canal. *(Edward Hickey)*

The turnpiking of local roads at the end of the eighteenth century and into the early nineteenth century also facilitated the movement of goods. A few toll houses still survive in the Black Country to remind us of this. This is the Littleworth Toll House on the Sedgley–Tipton road, photographed on 17 January 1983. *(Michael Hale)*

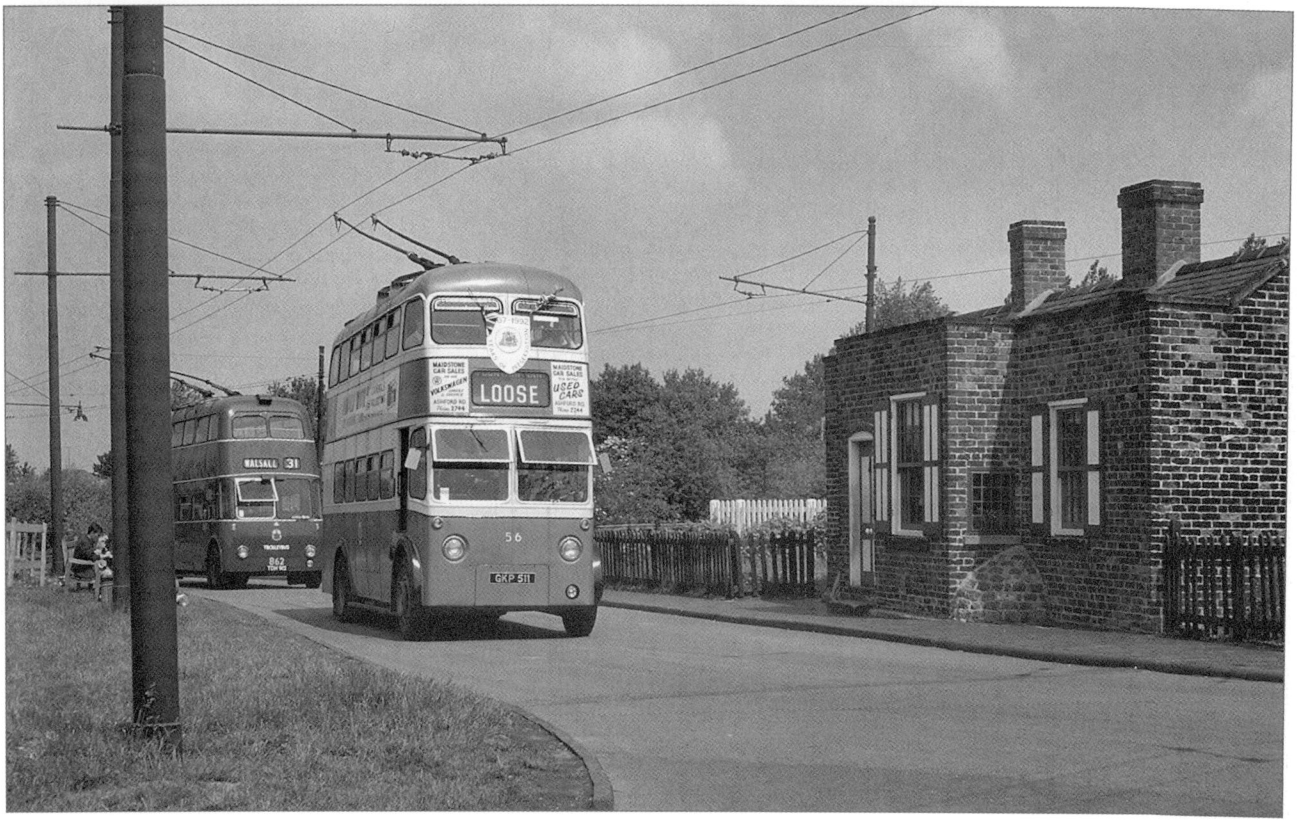

The Littleworth Toll House from Woodsetton has now been moved to the Black Country Living Museum. In recent years some very strange vehicles have passed its door. Here a Maidstone trolleybus, followed by one from Walsall, is about to pass the Toll House – all part of the 'Trolleybuses Galore' weekends that usually take place in June. *(Ned Williams)*

The tracks, lanes and turnpikes of the nineteenth century somehow had to develop into a road system fit for the twentieth century. When the electric tramways were laid along these roads at the beginning of the twentieth century they introduced the first really solid road surface. Here we see an open-top tram passing Holly Hall church on its way from Dudley to Stourbridge via Brierley Hill in the 1900s. *(Ken Rock Collection)*

St Augustine's Church at Holly Hall still guards this crossroads, but the main road has become a dual carriageway at this point. The traffic using this crossroads is now very heavy owing to its proximity to the Dudley Southern Bypass, Merry Hill, the general hospital at Russells Hall and so on. Road congestion is a major twenty-first-century problem for the region. *(Ned Williams)*

On 2 November 1927 the Wolverhampton–Birmingham 'New Road' was officially opened by the Prince of Wales, seen here cutting the tape at Oldbury UDC's boundary. It was a major local road-building initiative involving seven local authorities and utilising a 'corridor' of semi-derelict land. Early photographs show it almost devoid of traffic! *(Ken Rock Collection)*

Since the 1960s we have seen the arrival of the M6 and M5 motorways, followed in the 1990s by the opening of the Black Country Route and the Black Country Spine Road. We await further developments. On a quiet day in June 2002 the M6 at Junction 10 is caught in a fluid state! *(Ned Williams)*

The New Road of 1927 split Coseley in half, and to compensate for this some attractive gardens were laid out alongside it. The Clifton Cinema, partly obscured by a tree in this 1940s view, was opened on 8 July 1939. It closed on 10 August 1963. Note the absence of traffic on the New Road. *(Connie Walton)*

Returning to this location in 2002 it was *just* possible to capture a moment when the New Road seemed empty. The gardens are still tended, but the trees have grown and the Clifton Cinema has entirely disappeared. The new shops on the site are obscured by the trees. *(Ned Williams)*

Heavy haulage. Danks of Netherton made boilers and pressure vessels, many of which were large and had to be delivered by road. Here we see a steam road locomotive hauling a very long load about to leave Netherton in the late 1930s. *(Author's Collection)*

Today, large loads often make their way through the Black Country on Sundays to avoid meeting too much traffic. On Sunday 10 June 2001 this load has paused in Wellington Road, Dudley, before tackling the bends that lay ahead. *(Jim Houghton)*

The Black Country developed a good electric tramway network at the beginning of the twentieth century, and bus services came along in its wake. Midland Red, plus municipal transport provided by Walsall, Wolverhampton and West Bromwich Corporations created a dense pattern of services. This 1902 picture shows trams passing through Dudley Market Place to and from the terminus at the foot of Castle Hill, and a single-deck car in the terminal tracks in the foreground. *(Author's Collection)*

In 2002 Travel West Midlands painted two of its Dennis Trident Alexander-bodied double-deckers in a gold and purple Golden Jubilee livery. Here is no. 719 entering Wolverhampton bus station in July at the end of its journey from Walsall via Willenhall. *(Ned Williams)*

The Black Country has enjoyed the services of a profusion of coach operators. Wilf Kelsey of Bilston acquired just one coach from Don Everall in 1952 and it was his pride and joy for a short time. It was a 1938 AEC Regal, which had already enjoyed quite a chequered career before coming to Bilston. *(Wilf Kelsey Collection)*

On 12 May 2002 Wayne Powell prepares to drive Bill Whittaker's 'Old Bill' bus from the gates of Dartmouth Park, West Bromwich, down to the Sandwell Vintage Vehicle Rally. Bill Whittaker operates a fleet of coaches from his base in West Bromwich and also provides vintage vehicles for special occasions. *(Ned Williams)*

Langley Green station, 1902. It was a junction for the Oldbury branch, seen curving to the right in the foreground. The branch succumbed to competition from road transport, but the main line through Langley Green has become one of the busiest commuter lines in the Black Country, with frequent trains between Stourbridge Junction and Birmingham. *(Ken Rock Collection)*

Langley Green in June 2002 sports a new station building with an ornate clock tower. A commuter train is just departing for Birmingham. *(Ned Williams)*

Stourbridge Town station in the early 1900s. This was the terminus of one of Britain's shortest branch lines, opened in 1879 from Stourbridge Junction, less than a mile away. This postcard was produced by the local printers Mark & Moody. *(Ken Rock Collection)*

Against all the odds the Stourbridge Town branch has survived. A train is seen leaving the present station, adjacent to the bus station, in September 1997. The station has moved a few yards closer to the junction, and may move again if the Stourbridge ring road is rerouted in the near future. *(Ned Williams)*

The Stourbridge Town branch train can just be seen on the left of this view of Stourbridge Junction, as a 'Special' from Swindon comes through the station behind ex-GWR Dukedog class locomotive no. 9000 on 14 June 1953 – not long after the coronation. *(E.J. Dew)*

Jubilee year 2002 saw the 150th anniversary of the opening of the line from Evesham to Stourbridge by the Oxford, Worcester & Wolverhampton Railway. On 5 May Driver Mike Roberts prepares to depart with a special anniversary train carrying fare-paying excursionists and a civic party including the Mayor and Mayoress of Dudley (Mr and Mrs John Walters), and their opposite numbers from Droitwich and Evesham. *(Ned Williams)*

Happiness on wheels. Joe Horton took this picture of his wife Sylvia (left) and their friends on their BSA Goldstar motorcycles in about 1960. Joe and Sylvia were married in Bilston in 1957 after Joe had sold his motorcycle to buy an engagement ring. Although Sylvia had never been on a motorcycle before, she persuaded Joe to buy another one which they first used together on their honeymoon! *(Sylvia Horton Collection)*

Happiness for Leo and Hanny Greve from Naaldwijk in Holland is to jump on their Electra Glide motorcycle and head for the Black Country in their Highway Patrol uniforms. On July 2002 this enabled them to take part in a '999 Emergency Services' Rally held in Baggeridge Country Park. *(Ned Williams)*

Having Fun

The jazz band from Stringer's Tubular Holloware Company of Oak Street, Quarry Bank, ready to participate in the local carnival in the late 1920s. Carnivals have long been a traditional way of having fun and confirming a sense of local identity and community in the Black Country. Initially organised by churches and friendly societies, after the First World War they became the province of hospital committees. Since the Second World War they have raised money for a variety of charities. *(Brenda Holloway Collection)*

The Upper Gornal Carnival of 1926. The event was traditionally held before Lent. The girls on the float are representing the Mustard Club, promoted by Colman's Mustard. The girl just above the poster on the side of the lorry, then aged five, contributed the picture! *(Brenda Cartwright)*

Sitting on the back of a lorry is still the most fun. In Golden Jubilee year 2002 many floats were decorated with a St George theme. Here, floats enter the Memorial Park on 15 June 2002 as part of the Willenhall Carnival festivities. *(Ned Williams)*

A float at the 1974 Willenhall Carnival had the Carnival Prince and Princess sitting beneath a hastily constructed bower. Unfortunately this was still full of bugs, which then dropped on to the children throughout the procession! The float was decorated by a local photographer. *(Andrée Hickey)*

The Willenhall Carnival 'Munchkins' – James and Nicole Hall taking part in the procession on 15 June 2002. *(Ned Williams)*

The float assembled by workers at the Electric Construction Company for the Wolverhampton Carnival of 28 September 1918 took an autumn theme. Note the solid wheels of the truck. *(Author's Collection)*

The 8th Willenhall Brownies stuck to a jubilee theme for their float in the Willenhall Carnival of 15 June 2002. In recent times the number of local carnivals surviving in the Black Country has drastically reduced. Long-lived events like the carnivals in Lye, Wordsley, Quarry Bank and Lower Gornal have disappeared. Willenhall's continues, as do those at Bloxwich, Tipton and Wednesbury and a few others. *(Ned Williams)*

Carnivals need queens. Marianne Preece of Slim Road, Willenhall, was Carnival Queen at Bloxwich in 1965, and was *Wolverhampton Chronicle* Personality Queen in 1966. *(Marianne Roberts Collection)*

To celebrate the millennium several local carnivals assembled the carnival queens of the previous decade. On 17 June 2002 Willenhall Carnival Queen Leanne Marie Porter (seated left) is joined by assorted cherubs, princesses and queens from the previous decade. *(Ned Williams)*

Councillor Homer, Chairman of Brierley Hill UDC, opens the Quarry Bank Gala in Stevens Park in 1961. The three ladies in white behind him are, left to right, Pat Cox, Gala Queen Eileen Haddington and Maureen Hill. *(Eileen Thompson Collection)*

In October 1999 it was possible to restage this event thirty-eight years later as part of a local book-launching ceremony! Pat, Eileen and Maureen wear the tiaras and crown worn in 1961. Stan Hill, standing behind them, is currently President of the Black Country Society, but he was once Chairman of Brierley Hill UDC – and he wears the official chain of that office. *(John James)*

Miss P. Thompson became Wednesbury Carnival Queen in 1931 when the carnival was revived. Her attendants were Lily Doleman, Lily Palmer, Vera Sale and Miriam Smith. The picture was taken on 2 September 1931 in Wednesbury Town Hall after Miss Evelyn Laye, then appearing at the Wednesbury Hippodrome, had judged the contest. *(Ian Bott Collection)*

Elizabeth Skidmore was Carnival Queen for Lye Carnival on 22 August 1999. Her mother had once been Wordsley Carnival Queen, so it must run in the family! *(Ned Williams)*

Bilston Carnival, 1949. Mary Clarke, who ran the cake shop next door to the Odeon, crowns Joan Wilkes as Bilston Carnival Queen. Also present is the Mayor of Bilston, Councillor Edward Beards, a local headmaster. *(Joan Wilkes Collection)*

Lye's Millennium Carnival also lined up the queens from the previous decade. Here Geoff Phipps introduces them to the crowd on 20 August 2000, including the Millennium Queen herself, Rebecca Shepherd (third from right). The forecourt of Christ Church, Lye, provided an ideal venue for carnival rituals. Sadly the events have recently been abandoned. *(Ned Williams)*

Carnival Queen selection night in Bilston, 1949. Sylvia Timms, who is in the white dress, became Lady-in-Waiting to the girl on her left – Lucy Jones – who was crowned Queen. They are surrounded by judges and other contestants. *(Sylvia Horton Collection)*

On 22 May 2002 the Black Country Memories Club hosted a reunion for Bilston carnival queens. Left to right: Julie Evans, Margaret Jones, Mary Cox, Leanne Deeming, Christine Mills and Sylvia Horton (née Timms). *(Ned Williams)*

The larger Black Country carnivals were often in a position to ask a celebrity to come along and open the event. In 1974 we find 'Benny' from *Crossroads* at the Willenhall Carnival talking to Eddy and Andrée Hickey. They had been left to man Keith Bayley's photographic stand while Keith himself went to photograph the floats. A television star could help boost the attendance at carnivals – weather permitting! *(Andrée Hickey Collection)*

One has to admire the folks in 2002 who work so hard to keep carnivals alive without celebrities and sponsors, and often in small communities. On 13 July 2002 the promotors of the Bradley & Daisy Bank Carnival line up with their Carnival Queen, Kirsty Adams. *(Ned Williams)*

The Empire Jazz Band and others line up for the marching band contest held in Brunswick Park, Wednesbury, on the eve of the revived Wednesbury Carnival, September 1931. *(Frank Sharman Collection)*

In 2002 the Stourbridge Carnival benefits from being part of the Dudley Borough Festival, but even so, like other carnivals, it is finding it increasingly difficult to hold a parade. The marching band put on a good show in Lower High Street on Sunday 30 June 2002. *(John James)*

Many marching bands taking part in the 1931 Wednesbury Carnival band contest were works based – thus we discover that the Whoopee Girls were normally to be found at GKN's Alma Works. Today's marching bands are younger. *(Frank Sharman Collection)*

The Harlequin Eagles are a Willenhall-based marching band, and are therefore on home ground here as they assemble before leading the 2002 Willenhall Carnival procession off the Wakes Ground (now a lorry park) on 14 June 2002. Their route took them around the town to the Memorial Park. *(Ned Williams)*

The local brass band was a vital part of every urban community early in the twentieth century, growing out of the popularity of temperance movement bands and the bands assembled by friendly societies. Here is the Dudley Town Prize Band of the early 1900s. *(Author's Collection)*

The Langley Brass Band, based in Halesowen, is a popular band which has survived into the twenty-first century. Here its members are seen resting during a Sunday afternoon concert at the bandstand in Stevens Park, Quarry Bank, on 30 June 2002. Band concerts have now been revived in several local parks. *(Ned Williams)*

Above: Les Hatton playing the tenor sax at the Bulls Head, Wednesbury, *c*. 1955. He is pictured with Trevor Block, who later played with the Sid Lawrence band. Les subsequently joined the Royal Artillery Band and on returning to the Black Country combined the life of a professional musician with his work as a contract draughtsman. *(Les Hatton Collection)*

Above, right: By the 1990s opportunities for live music were much diminished, but Les was still to be found playing a baritone sax at the Trumpet in Bilston. In 2002 he describes himself as a retired musician – defeated by recorded music! *(Les Hatton Collection)*

Right: Three saxophonists of the twenty-first century. They form part of the St Peter's School Concert Band, Wolverhampton, seen here on 7 July 2002. *(Ned Williams)*

The Black Country produced its fair share of rock and roll bands. Here is Danny Cannon and the Ramrods – Bilston's greatest rock and roll group – taking the stage at a concert in the Gaumont Cinema, Wolverhampton, in the late 1950s. *(Express & Star)*

Affinity, a modern group from Walsall, photographed at the open day held at Bilston Street police station, Wolverhampton, on 31 July 1999. *(Ned Williams)*

Eddy and Pat Mattocks from Brierley Hill take to the floor in the 1950s. *(Eddy Mattocks Collection)*

Above and left: Rock and roll is alive and well, and features at a different venue virtually every night of the week in the Black Country of the twenty-first century. On Wednesday nights the action is at the Quarry Bank Labour Club. Some of the regulars cool off on 15 May 2002, before returning to the floor to swing their partners a few more times! *(Ned Williams)*

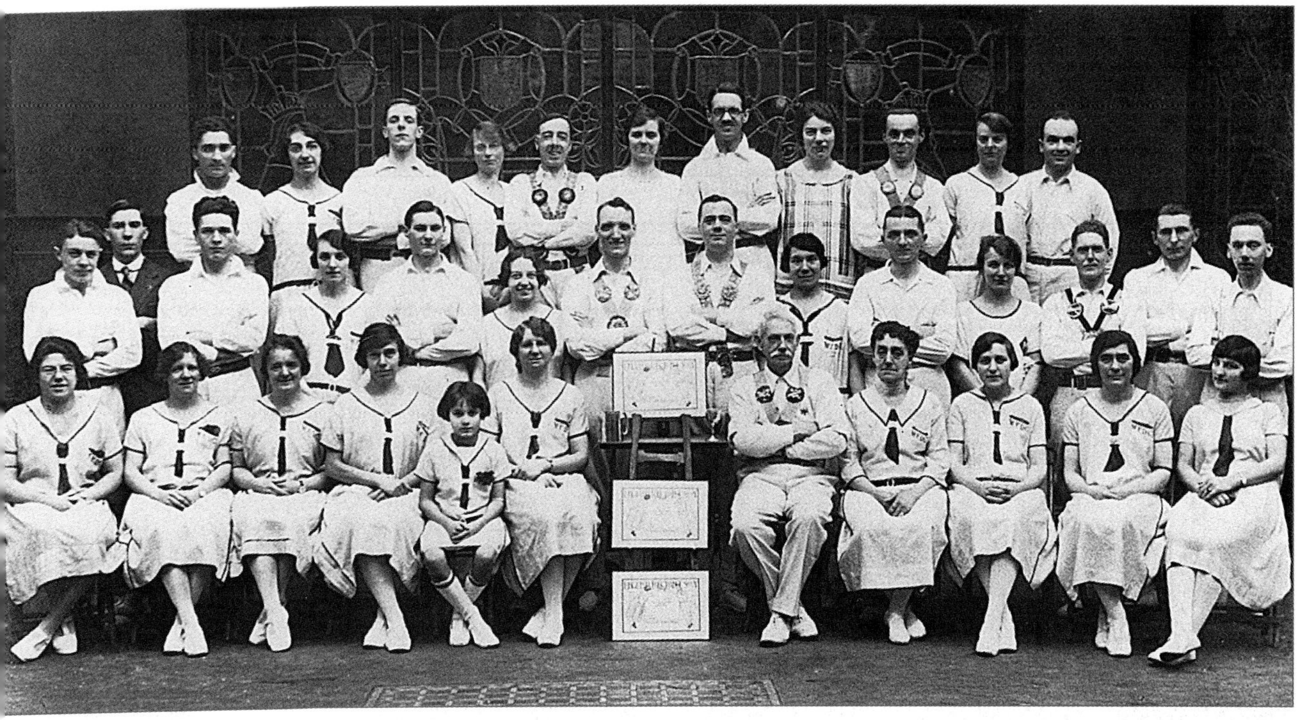

The Wulfruna Folk Dance Society seems particularly static in this picture taken in 1927 in the Queen's Arcade, Wolverhampton. *(Frank Sharman Collection)*

There's a little more movement here from the Castle Clog Dancers, demonstrating their skills at the Stourbridge Carnival on 30 June 2002. Like rock and roll, this dance form is probably an import to the Black Country. *(Ned Williams)*

Members of the Stourbridge Folk Dance Club, founded in 1978 by the late Des Willetts, photographed at the Mary Stevens/Age Concern Day Centre in Stourbridge. *(Trish Parsons)*

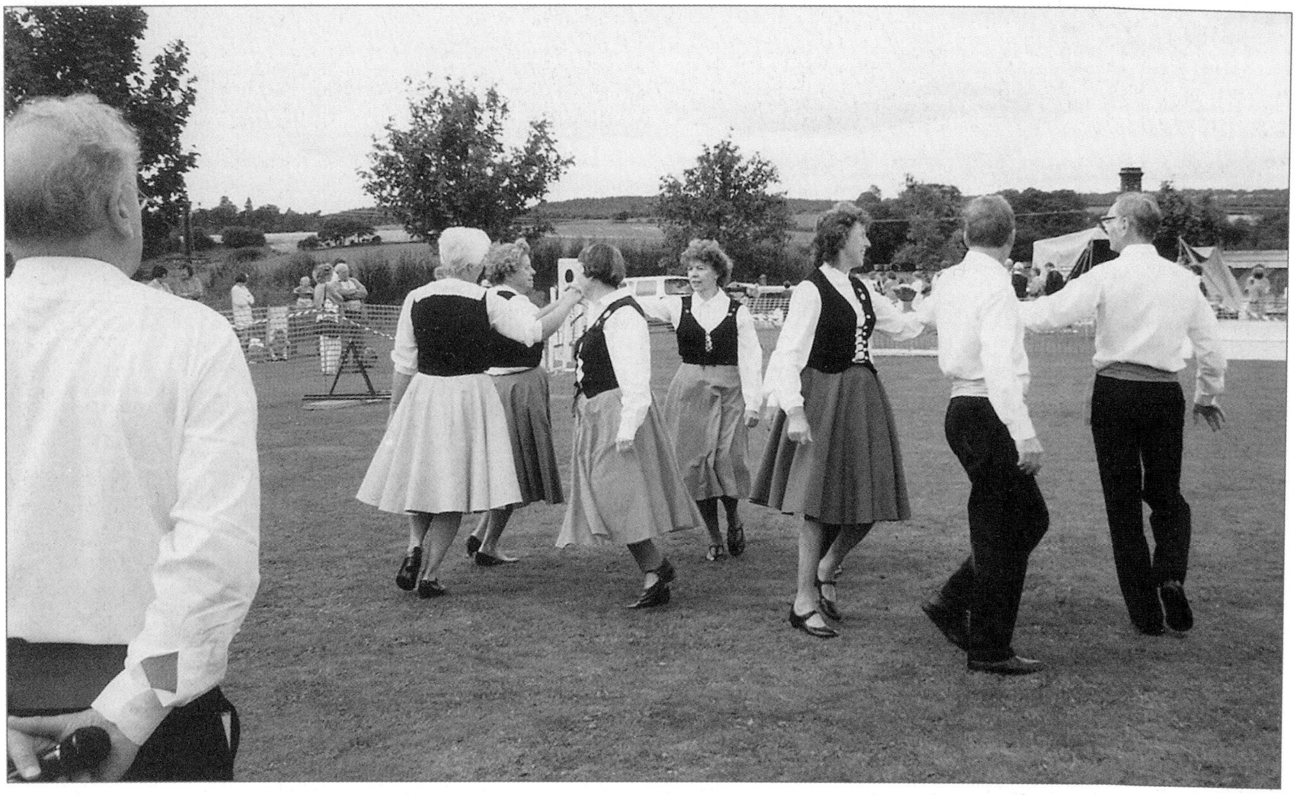

Des Willetts stands with his back to the camera as the club's dancers perform at Bobbington Fête in the 1990s. Susan Willetts, his wife, is in the centre of the picture. Since Des's death in 2000 she has been anxious to see the club keep going. *(Trish Parsons)*

The Stourbridge & District Scottish Dance Society was founded in 1952, and its members are seen here at an 'All Scottish' dance at Brierley Hill Civic Hall in 1964. They are dancing to Jimmy Shand and his band. The Mayoress of Stourbridge lost her chain of office while dancing the Eightsome Reel! *(Trish Parsons Collection)*

In recent times the Stourbridge & District Scottish Dance Society has performed for charities. Here they are dancing for the Real Aid Appeal at the Merry Hill Centre. *(Trish Parsons Collection)*

Local recreation for lads has long been 'swimming in the cut', and, as can be seen in this picture taken at Factory Junction locks, Tipton, on 9 June 1984, the tradition was still alive and well then. *(Jim Houghton)*

The Tipton Swimming Baths were a symbol of civic pride when they opened in the 1930s. In recent years their popularity had been revived when marketed as 'Costa del Tipton' to counter the 'Tipton on Cut' image. In 2002 they were threatened with closure, but this large demonstration was organised at a time when the baths were given a temporary reprieve, hence the 'We are open' banner. The dispute was often presented as a battle between the 'locals', the Tiptonians, and distant bureaucrats, Sandwell Council. The council argued it was providing many new sports facilities in Tipton and said the baths were under-used. The baths were suddenly closed just at the beginning of the 2002 summer school holidays. *(Express & Star)*

This picture of the founder members of Stourbridge Cycling Club, taken in about 1908, still hangs in the club's headquarters as a reminder of how cyclists ought to dress. *(Les Archer)*

Members of the Stourbridge Cycling Club present themselves rather differently in 2002. Here are members Richard Bowater, Barry Charles, Louise Robinson, Roger Iddles, Bob Couldrey, Isla Rowntree and Wayne Baker at the Merry Hill Centre for the opening of a new cycle path. On the left is their sponsor, Barry Adams, and on the right is Jeremy Rodway-Smith manager of the Merry Hill Centre. *(Express & Star)*

Did somebody mention football? Wolves fans in Trafalgar Square celebrate their team's success in 1949. *(Kathleen Burns Collection)*

This is what football fans look like today. Workers at the Bronx Engineering Works in The Lye are divided equally into Wolves and Albion supporters. *(Express & Star)*

The Black Country has never lacked places of entertainment. The Wood family came to Bilston in about 1910 and started showing films in the Town Hall. On 17 November 1921 they opened their grand purpose-built Wood's Palace, seen here. They provided full stage facilities as well as a cinema. The building, then an Odeon, closed in 1964. *(Angela Wood Collection)*

The building survived as a bingo hall and is now a banqueting hall, presenting itself as The Imperial Palace. Towards the end of 1999 Joe Boden (right) decided to relaunch live variety entertainment in Bilston and started regular Thursday night shows at the Palace. *(Ned Williams)*

The pantomimes presented at the Dudley Hippodrome were enormously popular. Here we see Jane Corda as Aladdin and Ruby Riggs as the Princess in the 1949 production of *Aladdin*. Theatres such as the Hippodrome brought the great theatrical stars of the day to the Black Country. *(Bob Hosier)*

Today only the Grand Theatre in Wolverhampton keeps professional theatre alive for Black Country audiences. But it's still an opportunity to meet the stars! Here we see Rob Walsh from Walsall queuing up to meet the stars of the 2002 pantomime at the Grand, *Snow White*. The stars include, from left to right: Graham Grumbleweed, Kathy Rooney and Paul Hendy. *(Ned Williams)*

When it came to cinemas, the Black Country had its share of Gaumonts and Odeons, Cliftons and Danilos, but the local Black Country 'bug hut' was much more modest. Cecil Couper of Brierley Hill built three little cinemas in the late 1930s – just the right size for the communities they served. At Netherton he built the Savoy, which opened on 26 August 1936 and is seen here decorated for the coronation in 1953. *(Mrs Bishop Collection)*

The latest cinema to open in the Black Country, our fourth multiplex, was the Showcase Cinema in Castle Gate, Dudley. This photograph was taken on the opening day, 12 October 2001. *(Ned Williams)*

When the circus came to town it was usually heralded by a parade. In July 1965 Billy Smart's elephants enter the Arboretum in Walsall, with Marianne Preece, Bloxwich's Carnival Queen, riding on the second elephant. *(Marianne Roberts Collection)*

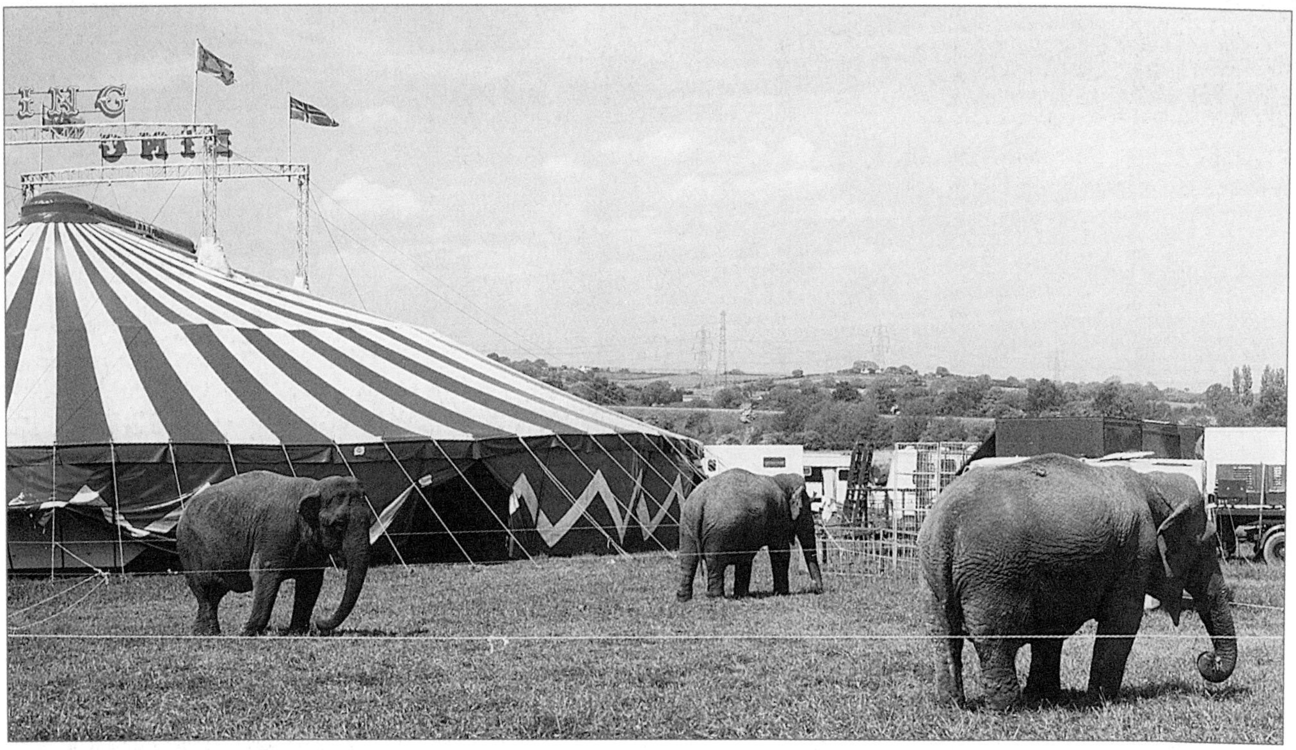

When the circus comes to town in the twenty-first century, it rarely includes any animals at all, let alone elephants. However, Circus King has kept the traditional animal acts in its programme and therefore we find elephants grazing at Wall Heath during their autumn 2000 visit. *(Ned Williams)*

Even a trip to the local library has changed. Here we see book-borrowers searching the shelves of Wednesbury Library in the 1950s. *(Wednesbury Library Collection)*

A trip to the local library in 2002 is not just about borrowing books. Jack Houlte from Tipton had come along to use the Internet when he was interrupted by the official opening of Wednesbury Library's new Learning Centre on 21 May 2002. Paul Voyce (left), Community Librarian, welcomes Lord King of West Bromwich, Mayor of Sandwell (right), to the Learning Centre – which used to be called the reading room. *(Ned Williams)*

Many Black Country folk expanded their horizons by joining uniformed organisations. Four of the 2nd Kingswinford Boy Scouts, founded in 1947, are seen here awaiting inspection while camping at Spring Grove near Bewdley in the late 1950s. *(Ray Hancock Collection)*

Scouts from the 4th Willenhall Troop, St Stephen's Church at Willenhall Carnival on 16 June 2002. Robert, Sue and Adam Cregeen show off the latest uniforms worn by Scouts and Leaders. *(Ned Williams)*

Mary Sidaway joined the Guides at the church in Dudley Wood, Netherton. She is seen here in about 1933. *(Mary Brookes Collection)*

Lucy Perry in her uniform as a member of the 1st Netherton Guide Troop. *(Jim Houghton)*

The 1st Rood End Group of the Oldbury Sea Scouts, 1950. *(Janet Seward Collection)*

Today's young people are more likely to look for a youth club. Captain Jenny Forman (right) lines up with members of the youth club meeting at the hall behind the Salvation Army Citadel in Field Street, Willenhall, in 2002. *(Captain Jenny Forman Collection)*

Many Black Country folk devote much of their own time to raising money for charity. Here we see the Walsall Lions presenting seven cots and a bed to the Manor Hospital in Walsall early in 1978. They had spent Silver Jubilee year collecting the money for this equipment. Third from the left is Graham Farr and on the right is Graham Wilton, still carrying out the Lions' motto 'We Serve' – in the picture below. *(Lions Collection)*

Walsall Lions at the Willenhall Carnival on 15 June 2002. Chairman Graham Wilton (left) was a founder member. *(Ned Williams)*

The stars and the Latour Girls (students at the local dance school) from the 1957/8 pantomime at Dudley Hippodrome collecting in Dudley Market Place for the Dog Rescue Fund just before Christmas 1957. On the right, with one of Cinderella's ponies, is Barry Foley. Next to him is the Mayor of Dudley, and next to the mayor is Derek Roy – star of the show. *(Barry Foley Collection)*

Still collecting money in Dudley Market Place in 2002 is Penny Benton, supporting the Salvation Army and selling *War Cry*. *(Ned Williams)*

What about the pensioners? On 30 June 1939 Councillor Arthur Smith of West Bromwich organised a pensioners' outing by coach to Sutton Park. Here they took a stroll, enjoyed the amusements provided by Pat Collins, and then were fed and entertained before going home with a carton of rock. *(Wilf Smith Collection)*

In January 2002 the Odeon at Quinton (previously known as the Danilo, Classic, ABC and so on) relaunched its pensioners' matinees. The minimal admission price includes refreshments and some shows have been so popular that people have had to be turned away. In this picture manageress Olga Ashley-Jones greets some prospective customers to show them round the cinema. *(Ned Williams)*

All the fun of the fair at Willenhall Wakes, one Sunday in September in the mid-1930s. The fair has closed but the crowds have gathered in front of Pat Collins' 'Dragon and Peacocks' to listen to the St Giles' Church Choir give a sacred music recital accompanied by the Wonderland organ in the depths of the ride. *(John Swallow Collection)*

Pat Collins' Wonderland organ survived when the ride was scrapped in 1962 and was put back on the road by Bill Hunt. On 10 August 2001 it was played in Bloxwich's King George V park in a special pre-carnival concert for senior citizens. Next to the organ stands a Scammell showman's tractor fully restored by Anthony Harris and his family, the present proprietors of Pat Collins' Funfair. *(Ned Williams)*

Jubilee

Street parties enjoyed good weather in 1977 when it came to celebrating the Queen's Silver Jubilee, as seen here in Gordon Drive, Tipton. *(Express & Star)*

In coronation year, 1953, extra carnivals and galas were held to celebrate the occasion and carnival queens, coronation queens and may queens all merged. Here we see Barbara Hipwell as a Carnival Queen, with a distinctly 'coronation' look, being greeted by the Chairman of the Senior Citizens Committee for whom the event had been organised in Lanesfield. *(Barbara Patrick Collection)*

In 2002 the Golden Jubilee was celebrated with much dressing up. This event was organised within Mount Pleasant Primary School, Quarry Bank. The Queen is Philippa Coley, attended by (left to right) Claire Hampton, Natasha Redfern and John Barnsley, marshalled by the head teacher, Mrs Gail Bedford. *(John James)*

The highest Silver Jubilee street party in the Black Country must have been the one organised at Oakham. Fancy dress is a key ingredient on these occasions. *(Express & Star/Mary Brookes Collection)*

Another key ingredient seems to be games. On 3 July 2002 we see the residents of Acres Road, Quarry Bank, grabbing some bin-liners for a sack race. *(John James)*

The most appropriate place to hold a Silver Jubilee party in the Black Country in 1977 was Jubilee Street in West Bromwich – which was probably named after the local pit which started life in the year of Queen Victoria's Diamond Jubilee, 1897. The street was well filled for the event. *(Express & Star)*

In 2002 it was much more difficult to obtain permission to close streets for parties, not to mention the need to leap other bureaucratic hurdles, so true street parties were much rarer. In Acres Road, Quarry Bank, residents used front gardens and garages rather than the road itself. The weather also forced organisers to exploit another modern device – the portable gazebo. *(John James)*

The main ingredient of a party is the food! Here we see the children of Turner Street, West Bromwich, sitting down to a feast to celebrate the coronation in 1953. *(Wilf Smith Collection)*

The Wrens Nest Residents Association, Dudley, had to deal with adverse weather in 2002 and so their Golden Jubilee Feast was held in the Community Centre in Summer Road, Dudley. *(Jim Houghton)*

Although jubilee street parties were primarily organised for children, the adults joined in the fun, and everyone seems to have felt that such events captured a sense of community that is often elusive at other times. This is certainly true of the local events of 1953, 1977 and 2002. Once again we turn to the residents of Turner Street, West Bromwich, to capture the spirit of 1953. *(Wilf Smith Collection)*

Plenty of red, white and blue among the organisers of the Wrens Nest Residents Association's 2002 Golden Jubilee celebrations. *(Jim Houghton)*

Pupils of Mount Pleasant Primary School, Quarry Bank, sitting down to enjoy the 1977 Silver Jubilee celebrations in the school playground. *(John James)*

In 2002 other, more dramatic, ways were devised to celebrate the Golden Jubilee. The children of Thorns Primary School in Quarry Bank, dressed in red, white and blue, released hundreds of red, white and blue balloons on 31 May 2002. The note attached to one was returned from Germany. *(John James)*

Black Country folk of all ages got together to celebrate the Queen's Golden Jubilee in 2002, as represented by these residents of Acres Road, Quarry Bank. *(John James)*

Acknowledgements & Picture Credits

Over the years a number of people have generously made photographs available to me. Some of these people have passed away, but I know they provided photographs in the hope that they would be shared via eventual publication. Others have responded at great speed specifically to my request for photographs for this publication.

Pictures have been credited to their source. This is not the same thing as saying that the photographs were actually taken by that person – they are simply prints in that person's collection. In this situation every effort is made to acknowledge fairly the use of each picture and respect people's proprietorial rights, whether the images be family snaps or commercial photographs. Some pictures are copied from postcards, and I thank Ken Rock and Ian Bott for making their postcard collections available to me. I also wish to thank the Editor of the *Express & Star* for allowing me to reproduce pictures which have appeared in that paper.

In the past I have been grateful for Jan Endean's great work with photographic negatives. It is a sign of the times, and changing technology, that recent projects have benefited from similar skills which people now bring to working with computers and scanners. Thanks to Wilf Smith and Suzie who have helped in this respect.

Many people contribute to a book such as this in a great variety of ways and I would like to thank the following, arranged in alphabetical order. I apologise to anyone who discovers that I have forgotten to mention them. I am also grateful to all those people who cooperated in the taking of present-day pictures:

Les Archer, Eileen Beards, Revd Graham Bennett, Margaret Bowdler, Mary Brookes, Charlemont Primary School, Pat Collins Funfairs, Harold and Iris Dale, Barry Foley, Jenny and Steve Forman, Mary Fowler, Michael Hale, Ray Hancox, Les Hatton, Andrée and Eddy Hickey, Jennifer Hill, Stan Hill, Keith Hodgkins, Sylvia Horton, Jim Houghton, John and Pam Hughes, Judi Hughes, Judith Hyde, John James, G.V. Jenkins, Midlands Co-operative Society, Mount Pleasant Primary School, Pat and Eddie Mattocks, David Nott, Phil Osborne, Trish Parsons, Glyn and Geoff Parton, Barbara Patrick, Terry Price, Marianne Roberts, Derek Saunders, Brian Seymour of West Bromwich Building Society, Mary Stevens, Mary Wallet, Connie Walton, Alan Watkins, Les Westwood, Dave Whyley, Susan Willetts, Graham Wilton, Margaret Woodhall.

RBAN
ARWAY